Be Restored!

GOD'S POWER FOR AFRICAN AMERICAN WOMEN

DEBRA BERRY

NEW HOPE
PUBLISHERS
Gospel-Centered. Missions-Driven.

BIRMINGHAM, ALABAMA

New Hope® Publishers
P. O. Box 12065
Birmingham, AL 35202-2065
NewHopeDigital.com
New Hope Publishers is a division of WMU®

Library of Congress PCN: 2013943559

ISBN-10: 1-59669-384-3
ISBN-13: 978-1-59669-384-5

N134125 • 0813 • 3M1

# DEDICATION

This book is dedicated to my parents: Sheldonia and the late Ernest Berry. Thank you sharing and modeling a faith that can overcome every obstacle.

TABLE OF CONTENTS

ACKNOWLEDGMENTS

Gratitude fills my heart as I recall the countless women who have shared with me their appreciation for the first edition of *Be Restored: God's Power for African American Women*. When New Hope Publishers voiced their desire to publish this anniversary edition of the book, I responded with excitement in the affirmative. My thanks to New Hope's staff for their patient efforts to see this new edition from conception to completion. Special appreciation goes to my editor, Joyce Dinkins, for walking me through every step of the process. My sisters Ernestine Mickens, Jessie Teresa Berry, and Patricia Brown continue to be my loving supporters. Our parents taught us to keep the faith and always stick together. All glory and honor is due and given to our Lord and Savior, Jesus Christ.

INTRODUCTION

African American sisters in Christ, our God did a marvelous thing when He ordained that we should live in the beginning decades of the twenty-first century. The wonderful gifts of faith that open any door, our cultural heritage, along with loving family and friends have shaped us into uniquely chosen vessels for this present age. What has been lost through life's struggles and circumstances must be reclaimed, taken back, and restored. Restored to become all that God's high favor bestows upon us will equal fulfilled lives, healthy families, vibrant houses of faith, and revitalized communities.

This Bible study is the outgrowth of the passion of my heart. My heart lines up with the passion of God to see His people fully restored—claiming and exercising the spiritual gifts that will restore our homes, churches, and community. I feel the groundswell of African American women like you who want to be restored. We need spiritual restoration. Personal restoration is not a single event—it is the commitment of a lifetime.

Our study for the next eight weeks outlines the story of Nehemiah, a servant who accepted God's calling to bring restoration to the people of Israel after they had been released from captivity. The similarities between the plight of Israel and our own people are at times stark. Some of their nation had achieved economic success in exile. Many were faithful followers of God. Yet too many were left behind longing for spiritual, social, economic, and psychological release—restoration. The people of Israel were physically free, but some were still locked in the prisons of hopelessness and despair. Some were financially successful but had lost their sense of purpose and destiny as the nation that was the people of God. Change the names and times, and their plight is like a description of African Americans in the beginning of this new millennium.

This newly revised edition of *Be Restored: God's Power for African American Women* includes profiles of historic and contemporary women of African descent whose lives have inspired others to keep the faith and restore their communities, nations, and world. Some of their stories may be familiar to you and others are stories that few have heard. Yet, their resolve to carry out their divine assignments affirms that all things are possible with and through God. They inspire me and I know their lives will inspire you.

This study is not to blame Black folk. We have endured and achieved against odds that would have destroyed those with less faith and determination. We have come this far by faith. Yet we must take responsibility for ourselves. We must fight against any tendency to rest on our laurels or past achievements. The race is not finished. The voice of the Lord and the voices of our God-fearing ancestors call us to continue the struggle for the restoration of our people. We can only do this by the might and power of the God who loves us.

We are not advocating or promoting separation or exclusion of peoples of different hues, who are equally the children of God. We must understand, however, that elevating and strengthening our people in Christ-centered ways will also strengthen the body of Christ, our nation, and our world.

BEFORE YOU BEGIN

This Bible study was written with you in mind! I hope it will awaken in your heart a determination to follow God's calling on your life.

In eight lessons we will learn how to move toward personal spiritual restoration. I hope you will be encouraged to begin or continue a lifelong work for God. We will consider how the story of Nehemiah relates to us and convicts us today to follow God's path toward restoration, something He deeply desires to give to us.

This Bible study covers the main portions of the Nehemiah story (Nehemiah 1–9 and 12). We end the lesson on a high note as Nehemiah and the people express vigorous praise because their city walls, gates, and spiritual lives have been restored. Their love and joy overflow because of what God has done! I hope this will be true in your life as well.

The ingredients of each week's lesson are as follows:
1. **Vital Verses** highlight the key focus of the lesson.
2. **Key Terms** increase your understanding of the week's Scripture passage and the study.
3. **Life experiences of African American Christian women** are addressed in the opening section of each lesson as well as in your transition to the Lesson Summation. You or your group may or may not agree with my assertions, but I hope they jump-start your thoughts on the topic of the week.
4. A **Scripture selection** for each lesson is provided to guide you into reading larger sections of the Book of Nehemiah.
5. Each lesson tells part of Nehemiah's life in **story** form. The stories will hopefully bring to life the ancient story of the restoration of Jerusalem and, occasionally, make you laugh. I love laughter, particularly the laughter of women of God!
6. **Questions** are provided within the lesson to help you interact with the Bible and see how the lesson applies to you.
7. The **Lesson Summation.** We will see contemporary and historical African American women, their choices and voices and their impact on others. Then the summation encourages *you* to commit and get involved. It will tie together the information shared in the week's study.
8. Each lesson has a **Daily Devotions** section that provides five bite-sized devotional suggestions to help you consider the topic with the aid of Scriptures, mostly in the New Testament.

Most importantly, begin each lesson by praying for the power of God's Holy Spirit to touch you and your group. Prayerfully consider each portion of the lesson as you study. End with a prayer for the persons and situations that God brings to your heart. Ask God to quicken your heart's desire to assist Him in restoring His people.

The Leader's Guide provides you with lesson plans if you plan to use *Be Restored!* as a group study. Invite your friends, co-workers, Sunday School class, Bible study group, or neighbors to join you in this study. I pray that all the women who study these lessons will be empowered and blessed. Sisters in Christ and by mutual cultural heritage, *be restored!*

In the Lord's joy,

Debra Berry

CALLED ~~TO~~ RESTORE

NEHEMIAH 1:1–4

VITAL VERSE

"They said to me, 'Those who survived the exile and are back in the province are in great trouble and disgrace. The wall of Jerusalem is broken down, and its gates have been burned with fire.'" —NEHEMIAH 1:3

KEY TERMS

Restore: To take back a possession, to reestablish or to recover one's spiritual wholeness (Psalm 23:3 and Psalm 51:12). In the Old Testament, restoration also refers to the reestablishment of the prosperity of the people and land of Israel following a time of devastation, such as the Babylonian exile (Jeremiah 29:14).

Gates/Walls: In ancient times, city walls or fortifications were used as protection from enemies or to launch attacks against one's enemies (Ezekiel 21:15, 22). Gates were especially protected with towers because to "possess the gate" was to possess the city (Genesis 22:17).

Covenant: An agreement or contract between two parties with each assuming some obligation. A person or nation with greater power may impose a covenant on a less powerful group. In Old Testament times, a more powerful nation might agree to protect a weaker nation in exchange for loyalty. Israel entered into the Sinai covenant, promising loyalty to God's Law in exchange for God's protection and blessings.

Babylonian Exile: The period in the sixth century B.C. when the Jewish people were captured and taken to captivity in Babylon. During this captivity, Persia defeated Babylon, and the Jews in exile were under the rule of the Persian Empire.

Kislev: In the calendar of Nehemiah's time, Kislev is a month that comes in the fall, around late November and early December (Nehemiah 1:1).

M̲y sisters in the faith and in African American heritage, when we first looked at the status of our communities through this study a decade ago, I wrote:

> The walls that protect and secure the future of our people are torn down and the gates burned with fire! Nehemiah heard this report in his day, and it echoes daily in reports on the state of Black America. Violent crimes continue to make our communities like war zones; as a result our children experience psychological symptoms like the children of war-torn nations. Fifty percent of all children killed with firearms are Black. The number one cause of death among Black males 18 to 34 is gunfire. When I hear this, I hear, *our walls are torn down and our gates are burned with fire.*

Ten years ago, I wrote: When I read reports that more Black males are going to jail than to college, I see, *our walls are torn down and our gates are burned with fire.* When the Centers for Disease Control reports that the fastest growth rate in HIV/AIDS infection is among African American men and women (41 percent of all cases), can't you hear, *our walls are torn down and our gates are burned with fire?* More than 50 percent of Black children are reared in often financially struggling single-parent homes. One in five African American teenage girls becomes pregnant each year. The Children's Defense Fund tells us that 30 percent (3.5 million) of our children live in poverty. *Can't we see that our walls are torn down and our gates are burned with fire*?

Health experts tell us that we report higher rates of stress due in no small part to being born Black females in America—partly because of our desire to rear children that succeed in a racially biased society. Such day-to-day demands lead to stress-related illnesses, like hypertension and heart disease, and even to early graves. *Don't we know that our walls are torn down and our gates are burned with fire?*

Sunday School teachers tell us that we are so busy keeping up with the Joneses, we don't study the life of Jesus Christ. Preachers tell us we are so busy getting stuff—cars, houses, clothes, position, status—and trying to keep the stuff we got, we don't give God first place in our hearts, minds, and souls.

Regardless of some shifts in statistics, the long and the short of it is, we remain under siege, assault, attack from external and internal forces that we—strong, caring, and gifted women that we are—cannot surmount, overcome, address, handle all by *our bad Black selves*. The Book of Nehemiah in the Bible shows us that the people of Israel, a century after their Babylonian captivity, were in the same dreadful situation we find ourselves in more than a century after our emancipation from American captivity. Many of us have survived and done well, yet many of us have a very long way to go.

Nehemiah's response to the news of his people's torn-down walls and burned gates—their devastation, hopelessness, and vulnerability—was to let go of every lesser priority and seek the face and favor of God. He humbled himself and prayed; he waited patiently until he heard from heaven; he exercised childlike faith; then he obeyed the awesome God of Abraham and Sarah, Isaac and Rebecca, Jacob and Rachel. Absolute confidence in, total dependence on, and child-like obedience to God through faith in Jesus Christ the Son is our pathway to restoration, renewal, rebirth, and revival for ourselves, our people, our nation, and our world!

How have we had an impact to rebuild our communities and nation, our world in the last decade?

What remains in our efforts to rebuild our communities, our nation, our world in this present decade?

Walk with me as we survey the life and times of Nehemiah to collect spiritual timber, tools, and bricks that will continue to restore our spiritual lives, continue to rebuild African American communities, and continue to transform our world for Christ until He comes.

THE BOOK OF NEHEMIAH

Nehemiah, this leader of the fourth century B.C., will challenge us to be faith-inspiring, God-fearing, people-serving African American women of the twenty-first century A.D. Come with me as we get the facts of Nehemiah's life from his memoirs, a semiautobiographical diary found in these segments of the Old Testament book bearing his name: Nehemiah 1–7; 12:27–43; and 13:4–31. We'll see how God empowered Nehemiah to bring restoration to his devastated homeland and how he battled internal and external obstacles as he led the rebuilding of the walls and gates of Jerusalem.

This story takes place in a crucial time in Israel's history. The Book of Nehemiah finishes the story begun in 1 Chronicles and

2 Chronicles, which contain the history of Israel just before the Babylonian captivity. The Book of Nehemiah is closely related to the Book of Ezra—both books tell the story of the rebuilding of Jerusalem after Persia defeated Babylon and gradually released the Jews from captivity. Scholars believe an anonymous author compiled the books of Ezra and Nehemiah from their memoirs. This author, often called the Chronicler, may have been the same one who wrote Chronicles. The earliest record of the Book of Nehemiah treats it not as a book on its own but as "Volume Two" of the Book of Ezra. For this study, we'll focus on the memoirs of Nehemiah.

Take time now to read this week's main Scripture, Nehemiah 1:1–4.

NEHEMIAH THE MAN

If any Israelite had his act together and future assured, it was Nehemiah. His true-life drama depicted in the book that hears his name began while he was serving in the coveted position of cupbearer to King Artaxerxes I of Persia. It was the spring of 444 B.C., and Nehemiah was living well in the midst of the wealth and grandeur of Persia. His place of employment was the luxurious winter palace, located in Susa. In royal processions, the cupbearer to the king walked in front of the bearer of royal weapons and just behind—get this—the crown prince. He had two major duties: he tasted the king's wine and was guardian of the royal apartment. While doing so, he wore the finest clothes and ate the best cuisine; there were no "budget gourmet" chefs in the palace.

Nehemiah was entertaining his brother, Hanani, and friends from Jerusalem (Nehemiah 1:1–2). Some scholars speculate that Hanani and his friends were a formal delegation from Nehemiah's motherland. Their purpose may have been to share with Nehemiah the dire, grim, awful state of affairs there. Perhaps when they got there and saw the wealth and grandeur of Persia and the high position and lavish life of their friend and brother, they forgot why they had come to Susa in the first place. Surely, what they saw and heard left their mouths *hanging wide open.*

We can only imagine the joy they and Nehemiah felt and the tears that were shed at that meeting. They must have been glad to be together again. Some 150 years earlier, their war-torn nation was defeated and devastated by the invading Babylonian army. The forebears of Nehemiah were marched out of Jerusalem, stripped of their possessions and loved ones, exiled from the only life they had ever known. Would there be a future for them? Nehemiah's life, position, and circumstance were testimonies to the goodness, mercy, and love of God.

In the midst of their laughter and tears, Nehemiah showed us his heart. He asked his homeboys, "How are things, how are the *people* that survived the captivity, and how is the *land*?" Often when shocking news is about to be shared, the one sharing the news has the foresight to tell the recipient to sit down, "'cause what I'm about to say is goin' to knock you off your feet." Somebody in the delegation should have told Nehemiah to sit down. What they shared with Nehemiah floored him—knocked him off his feet.

Their answer to Nehemiah's concerned question is found in our Vital Verse for this lesson, Nehemiah 1:3: "They said to me, 'Those who survived the exile and are back in the province are in great trouble and disgrace. The wall of Jerusalem is broken down, and its gates have been burned with fire.'" A tidal wave of emotion flooded Nehemiah. He wrote, "I sat down and wept" (v. 4). His legs weakened and his body trembled as he began to cry uncontrollably and a feeling of deep sadness overtook him. Josephus, the great Jewish historian, described the situation in Jerusalem at that time in these words:

> *The surrounding nations were inflicting many injuries*
> *on the Jews, overrunning the country and plundering it*
> *by day and doing mischief by night, so that many had*

been carried off as captives from the country of Jerusalem
itself; and every day the roads were found full of corpses.

This news was like a knife through Nehemiah's heart. Nehemiah expected glowing news about Jerusalem. Some 150 years had passed since their defeat by Babylon. About 100 years earlier, a decree of Persian King Cyrus had allowed Jewish exiles to return and rebuild their lives in the former city of David. At Cyrus's decree, tens of thousands had returned and begun to rebuild. But in the meantime, though there were many victories and spiritual reforms, times were still tough in Jerusalem.

Unlike today, news back then traveled slowly. There was no email, cell phones, or CNN. Maybe Nehemiah had only received the Persian news carriers' sanitized version of the happenings in Jerusalem. When his brother Hanani visited, Nehemiah heard the real deal from eyewitnesses to and participants in the struggle.

Maybe Nehemiah vaguely recalled the stories of the sufferings of his people, but many Jewish exiles of his generation had not heard of the fate of Jerusalem since the Babylonian Captivity. Many middle-aged and younger African American people are only vaguely aware of our ancestors' struggle out of slavery, through the promise of reconstruction, the backlash of Jim Crow, and the sufferings and triumphs of the civil rights movement. Many more of us just reap the harvest provided by those who sacrificed their blood, sweat, and tears. We have reaped the benefits but have forgotten the huge price they paid. Some of us were eyewitnesses to and participants in our Black American struggle for dignity and freedom.

THE SUFFERINGS OF THE PEOPLE

Perhaps you were like me, a Black female child in the racially separated, deeply divided, immensely unequal environment of the Deep South of the 1960s. As a school-age child in a working-class neighborhood (Rosemont) of Charleston, South Carolina, I heard the conversations of my elders as they declared their allegiance to Dr. Martin Luther King Jr., and the movement he led. I saw the pride in the faces of my parents, Ernest and Sheldonia, when Dr. King and others articulated the cries of our people—a people to whom justice had been denied. I recollect our fears and tears when students on the predominantly Black campus of nearby South Carolina State University were killed during their nonviolent protest. My aunts were students at the school, and we feared for their safety.

After the death of Dr. King, I recall the low whispers and weeping of teachers and fellow students at Corbitt Edwards Elementary School. For weeks prior to his death, we had rehearsed the wrapping of the May Day pole. Our annual May Day celebration was canceled for fear of racial violence against innocent children on their school playground. Even today as I write these memories, tears pass down my cheeks, and I wonder at the cruelty of the sin of racism. Yet because of the faith of my parents and other God-fearing Black folk, I believe in the ultimate liberation of my people through the awesome, just, powerful God of love we serve.

Nehemiah had "arrived" in Persia through his role as cupbearer to the king. A member of a minority group, he served with rank, privilege, and distinction in "the big house"—the biggest house. Yet he was accessible, available, approachable; he hung around the king but he kept the common touch. I like Nehemiah, don't you? He had it all, but he cared about those who did not have anything. He was placed in a high position, and he understood what many forget: "to whom much is given, from him much will be required" (Luke 12:48 NKJV).

When Nehemiah learned the status of his homeland and people, the news tore into his heart and knocked him off his feet. He then moved from his sitting position to a kneeling position—he went to God in prayer. He stayed in prayer seeking God's face and favor until he heard from God. His answer was a call from God to be an advocate and leader of his people. His parents probably didn't know, maybe they had prayed, that their son Nehemiah, whose name means "the Lord comforts," would prophesy the fulfillment of God's promise to comfort His people.

WALL AND GATES

The glorious past of Israel was a bitter dream in the hearts and minds of the Israelites left in Jerusalem. When kings David and Solomon ruled, the Israelites rivaled the great kingdoms of the world, but at this point, the great city was without a wall and gates; it had no defense or protection. Violent crimes ruled the streets. Many who dwelt there lacked the necessities of life. They were easy targets for their enemies. The citizens were ashamed of their situation. The broken-down wall and burned gates left them prey to the impurities of the religious practices of the nations that surrounded them.

Visualize the status of the spiritual wall and gates that surround you and your family. Is the wall and are the gates strong and fully secure? Are they under siege?

What are the first steps you should take to reinforce or rebuild the wall and gates? (See Psalm 27:7–14.)

Consider current dilemmas that confront our economically depressed communities, including high teen pregnancy rates, HIV/AIDS, males and females in prison, underemployment, unemployment, and youths committing suicide. Many Blacks who have experienced greater economic success in America still meet resistance and are denied opportunities based on their race or gender. Others want, reject, lack, or have lost a committed relationship with Jesus. And all of us struggle with the world's demands on us versus the things of God.

Visualize the status of the wall and gates that surround Black America. Is the wall and are the gates strong and fully secure? Are they under siege? (See Psalm 27:1–6.)

For example, when African American youth and White youth are charged with the same crime, minority youth are five times more likely to be detained. These African American children aged 10 to 17 are much more likely to be charged as adults and sent to prison. Yet we still believe that all things are under the power of God. We must ask ourselves what we will do to make a difference. Can we do more?

What are the first steps we should take to reinforce or rebuild the wall and gates? (See Hosea 10:12 and Luke 11:10.)

Visualize the status of the spiritual wall and gates that surround the United States. Most Americans, when polled, state that they are Christians. Is the wall and are the gates strong and fully secure? Are they under siege?

What are the first steps we should take to reinforce or rebuild the wall and gates? (See 2 Chronicles 7:14.)

Nehemiah's response to Jerusalem and his people's plight tugs at our heartstrings even today. He sat down, wept, mourned, fasted, and prayed (Nehemiah 1:4). Like the psalmist, he sought the face of God. The face of God is the place where the presence of God resides. Dwelling in God's presence implies an urgent desire to gain God's favor. It means a willingness to lay our situation and ourselves at the foot of the throne of God. It demands a banishment of all pretense and pride. When personal or group sin is part of the problem, it requires godly sorrow and a decision to turn away.

Nehemiah was living well in Persia, but his heart was broken for his nation. Nehemiah went to the source of mercy, love, strength, and wisdom—the God of Israel. Seeking God's face was a pattern of Nehemiah's life. Throughout his ministry in Jerusalem, he sought God's guidance through prayer. The first step to ensuring that our wall and gates are secure is to go to the ultimate source of mercy, love, power, and wisdom. *This is where restoration begins.*

ISRAEL: THE CHOSEN PEOPLE

How did Israel get into its predicament? The Israelites were the chosen people of God. Countless times during their history as a nation, God had delivered them from their enemies.

Why was Israel selected as the chosen people? (See Genesis 12:1–3.)

Yes, God had done all these things. But Israel's favored status gave them a false sense of security. They began to feel that God would never allow their destruction. They failed to heed the cries of the prophets who warned of punishment unless they turned away from their sins. They listened to the prophets who told them what they wanted to hear.

Unless we acknowledge that bad things do happen to good people, we are naïve. However, the Scriptures and life itself prove that straying from the truths of God has negative consequences. We reap what we sow; what goes around, comes around. Israel's tendency to forsake the things of God came from a recurring malady: spiritual forgetfulness. They forgot that their past victories came from an absolute reliance on God. They forgot that they were the chosen people of God. They forgot their promise to keep their covenant with God. Israel promised at Sinai to be faithful to God. Instead they imitated the culture and the religious practices of those who worshipped false gods—false gods that promised the good life.

What would be consequences of the disease of spiritual forgetfulness for Israel? (Read Deuteronomy 6:10–19.)

Believers in Jesus have been called and chosen by God. Several Scriptures describe who we are as believers in Jesus Christ.

Read Ephesians 1:3–10 and 1 Peter 2:4–10, and summarize who you are as a believer in Jesus Christ.

Wow! We are chosen, precious, spiritual houses, holy priests, people of God, living stones, a holy nation, daughters of God, and redeemed!

Let's remind one another and ourselves of the wonderful ways God has chosen us. Forgetting leaves us easy prey to our spiritual enemy. When we remember, God gets the credit and we are empowered to live our purpose and calling in the world. *That's another avenue to our spiritual restoration.*

PERSONAL RESTORATION

In Psalm 27, the psalmist cried out to God for personal spiritual renewal and rebirth. No matter how far we stray away from God, if we turn away from sin, God will readily restore to us the joy of our salvation. God is faithful and promises to cleanse us of all of unrighteousness (1 John 1:8–10).

How does the availability of God's forgiveness help you when you have fallen prey to sin?

Often we need to return to giving God the first place in our lives. We must make this decision each moment we live. Frequently, our lives become unruly and out of balance. Selfish aims, work demands, family pressures, financial hardships, and poor time management, even church work deprive us from focusing on relationship with God. The result is that we become stressed or depressed.

How can we obtain forgiveness and restoration? (See 1 John 1:8–10 and Matthew 11:28–30.)

NEW COVENANT OF LOVE

The new covenant of Jesus Christ is written on the tablets of our hearts (Jeremiah 31:31–34). Yes, our salvation and eternal life are gifts of God through faith in His Son, Jesus Christ. Our faith is expressed in love for God and our fellow human beings—evidence of our Holy Spirit–empowered efforts to imitate Jesus Christ. The simple standard that will measure our commitment to our faith can be found in the reply of Christ to the question, "What is the greatest commandment?" Jesus responded by stating that God requires that our love for Him be the first priority and aim of our lives (Mark 12:29–30). Such love of God is expressed as we devote our minds, hearts, souls, and strength to God.

Does your lifestyle—manifested in the use of your time, talents, and resources—illustrate the magnitude of your love for God?

Secondly, we are to love our neighbors as we love ourselves (Mark 12:31).

How is love for your neighbor expressed in the use of your time, talents, and resources?

God has been faithful to us. We have survived the horrors and brutality of the Middle Passage, slavery, reconstruction, Jim Crow, and the civil rights movement. Throughout these times God has been "our rock in a weary land, our shelter in the time of storm." Israel's failure was the worship of idols and the imitation of the nations that surrounded them.

How faithful have we been to our vows to the Lord?

Love for our neighbor expresses itself in our willingness to share the blessings of God with others. Jesus stated that the way we treat the "least of these [people]" is the way we treat Him (Matthew 25:31–46).

Do we apply this rule in our encounters with people we consider undeserving as well as those that we consider deserving?

We must daily engage in the spiritual disciplines of prayer, study, worship, praise, and sacrifice to secure the strength of our wall and gates. God provided and provides the avenue to restoration through confession and repentance when we stray away from Him. We rejoice in the God of love and mercy whom we serve.

Septima Poinsette Clark, growing up under the watchful eyes of caring parents, herself quietly served the "least of these," day and night, and her steady sacrifice resounded in significant steps to build up the young and old—and ultimately the nation and world, even unto this time.

SEPTIMA POINSETTE CLARK

A US educator and civil rights activist, Sister Clark began her work for equal access to education and civil rights for African Americans decades before broadcast of racial inequality seared the nation's conscience. Clark's work garnered little recognition, but was essential, and her tireless work led to the acknowledgment that she is the "Queen mother" or "Grandmother" of the US civil rights movement.

Septima was born May 3, 1898, in Charleston, South Carolina, second of eight children to an illiterate former slave father, and a somewhat-educated mother. Her parents strongly believed in the importance of education. They desired and insisted that their children attend school. It was Mrs. Poinsette who insisted that Septima attend high school at Avery Normal Institute, a private school established by missionaries to educate African American children—as there were no public high schools available to Negroes. After graduating in 1916, Septima began working as a school teacher, although she was unable to attend college because she was financially unable to do so.

Because she was African American, she was not allowed to teach in Charleston, South Carolina public schools; so she found a position teaching on John's Island, a rural school district. She began—with children by day and illiterate adults by night—teaching and developing innovative systems to quickly help adults learn to read and write. Her systems used everyday materials, including the Sears catalog, for lessons.

The gross inequities of pay that existed between the black school and the white school led Mrs. Clark to become active in civil rights. She became an active proponent for equal pay for teachers, and joined the ranks of the NAACP (National Association for the Advancement of Colored People). It was her involvement with this organization that cost her her teaching job in 1956, when she refused to disavow her membership, and was subsequently fired. Afterwards, she worked for the Highlander Folk School, helping to set up Citizenship Schools throughout the South where black adults could learn to read and prepare to vote.

In the 1960s she worked with the Southern Christian Leadership Conference and was a close associate of Martin Luther King Jr. Clark and countless other women organizers risked their lives daily to perform the hard task of organizing work to persuade other blacks to risk life, limb, livelihoods, and housing to become involved to overthrow Jim Crow laws.

Mrs. Clark was not only a teacher, but was also a prolific writer of books and essays, giving talks on civil rights, race, racism, nonviolence, God and religion, American youth, and writing tributes to individuals and more topics. In addition to her other writings, and activism, she wrote materials about Old Bethel Methodist Church, Charleston, South Carolina, the church she attended and worked in during her later years.

LESSON SUMMATION

By the rivers of Babylon we sat and wept
when we remembered Zion.
There on the poplars
we hung our harps,
for there our captors asked us for songs,
our tormentors demanded songs of joy;
they said, "Sing us one of the songs of Zion!"
How can we sing the songs of the LORD
while in a foreign land?
If I forget you, O Jerusalem,
may my right hand forget its skill.
May my tongue cling to the roof of my mouth
if I do not remember you,
if I do not consider Jerusalem
my highest joy.

— PSALM 137:1–6

The feelings of the Jewish exiles in Babylon were expressed in Psalm 137. When Nehemiah learned of the devastation of his homeland, his response was to seek God's face. He went into the presence of God, seeking God's favor and comfort and asking direction. The deep pain he felt radically changed the direction of his life. His love for God and God's people would give him life to rebuild the wall and gates.

We are called to be restored. God has chosen and called each of us. God has called us to love. Each day we must seek God's face and answer God's call on our lives. We wait for the time when Christ will restore the heaven and earth to express and carry out the will of God.

ꝏDAIꝏDEVOTIONS

LESSON ONE
BUILDING BLOCKS FOR YOUR WALL AND GATES

Spend this week taking inventory of your spiritual wall and gates. Listed below are building blocks in the spiritual wall and gates of believers in Jesus Christ. Ask God to open your eyes and heart to areas where you need improvement. End your time in God's Word with a prayer for God's mercy, direction, and power.

DAY ONE

Building Block: Prioritizing a relationship with God
(Luke 10:27; John 21:16)

Building Block: Pursuing holiness
(John 14:15; Matthew 5:6; Job 4:17)

Do I possess these building blocks in my life?

What do I need to do?

DAY TWO

Building Block: Practicing Christ's love
(Matthew 25:31–46)

Building Block: Praying without ceasing
(James 5:15–18; Mark 11:20–26)

Do I possess these building blocks in my life?

What do I need to do?

DAY THREE

 Building Block: Praising God consistently
(Romans 12:1; John 4:24)

 Building Block: Partnering with citizens in God's kingdom
(Romans 12:9–21; John 13:13–35)

Do I possess these building blocks in my life?

What do I need to do?

DAY FOUR

 Building Block: Producing fruits of the Spirit
(John 15:1–2; Matthew 7:16)

 Building Block: Performing your spiritual gifts
(1 Corinthians 12; Romans 12:3–7; Ephesians 4:1–16)

Do I possess these building blocks in my life?

What do I need to do?

DAY FIVE

 Building Block: Proclaiming your faith in God
(Matthew 28:16–20; Luke 4:18–19)

 Building Block: Putting your resources in kingdom coffers
(Matthew 6:19–24; Malachi 3:6–12; 2 Corinthians 8:1–15)

Do I possess these building blocks in my life?

What do I need to do?

LESSON TWO

#
DESPERATE FOR GOD

NEHEMIAH 1:4–11

VITAL VERSE

"When I heard these things, I sat down and wept. For some days I mourned and fasted and prayed before the God of heaven." — NEHEMIAH 1:4

KEY TERMS

Prayer: Communion with God that includes conversation and awareness of God's presence. Prayer for the believer includes adoration, praise, thanksgiving, petition, and confession. Prayer on behalf of others is intercession. Prayer is empowered when we pray with pure lives and hearts (Matthew 6:1–2) and in the will of God (Matthew 26:39). With these things in mind, anything we ask in Christ's name will be done (John 16:23).

Covenant Love: God expresses the magnitude of His love for Israel through His faithfulness to His covenant with them (Nehemiah 1:5). Some translations use the words *steadfast love* to refer to God's faithful, covenantal love.

Favor: Nehemiah asks for God's favor before he seeks the favor of the king (Nehemiah 1:11). In Israel's history, God caused significant people to show favor to His people (Exodus 3:21; Exodus 11:1–2; Genesis 39:2–6). God also shows favor—good will, a preference for them—to people like Jesus' mother, Mary, and others (Luke 1:30;

Acts 7:46). The greatest desire of the believer is to have God's favor (Psalm 30:5; Psalm 84:11).

What do you do when you don't know what to do? "PUSH! **P**ray **U**ntil **S**omething **H**appens!" My sisters, the supreme power source of the believer is prayer. Yet prayer is the most underutilized tool in the Christian life. We have convinced ourselves that we do not have time enough to pray. Truth is, we do not have enough time *not* to pray.

We will not be restored until we get desperate for the ways of God. We must become desperate enough to let go of, push back from, cast aside anything and anyone that comes ahead or instead of communion with God. God is leaning over the balcony listening for our prayers — ready, willing, and able to rescue and revive us again. When we pray with faith, sincerity, and consistency, the power of God will flow in us and through us; we will speed up the time when God will rule in us and reign on earth as He does in heaven.

The testimonies of our ancestors declare that God is a lawyer in a courtroom, a doctor in a sickroom, a father to the fatherless, and a mother to the motherless. We would be arrogant and naïve to believe that we would be free citizens without our ancestors' faith-filled prayers. We now experience Christ's hope, peace, and joy because, with broken hearts and tear-stained cheeks, they for prayed us. Their sincere prayers for our deliverance were heard and answered by God. We are duty-bound to pray for the spiritual, social, and economic deliverance of future generations. We must be desperate for God.

Nehemiah was desperate for God. The report on the status of his people and homeland shook him at the core of his being. Nehemiah was doing well by the world's standards. As cupbearer for King Artaxerxes of Persia, he was in the inner circle of one the most powerful rulers on earth. He knew the movers and shakers of his day. He was "all of that and a bag of chips" with soda pop on the side. Yet Nehemiah knew that his problems would require the help of someone more powerful than King Artaxerxes. Nehemiah needed the ruler of the universe.

Prayer was as natural to Nehemiah as was breathing. At every point in his journey to Jerusalem's restoration, he relied on prayer. The key ingredient in the restoration of the spiritual and physical walls was Nehemiah's connection through prayer to the Most High God.

What do you do when you don't know what to do? Nehemiah knew the answer: "Go to the rock of our salvation!" Let's go to the text to find out from Nehemiah some principles for a powerful prayer life.

Take time now to read this week's main Scripture, Nehemiah 1:4–11.

NEHEMIAH, MAN OF PRAYER

Surely the rumor mill was turning, and gossip in the palace was that Nehemiah had changed. The fine clothes he was wearing seemed heavier. He smiled less often after he heard the shocking news of his people and homeland. Nehemiah was desperate for God. He did the best thing we can do when a situation sends our world wheelin' and rockin'—he prayed. Prayer is the thread that held his life together. When he lay down at night, his lips and heart were open to God. When he awoke from restless sleep, he lifted up holy hands in prayer. During the day while carrying out his duties, he whispered silent prayers. When the pace of the day slowed, he quietly went into his "prayer closet." He prayed constantly (as we are urged to do in 1 Thessalonians 5:17).

The Book of Nehemiah is a tribute to the might of prayer. From the moment he first learned of the crisis in Jerusalem, Nehemiah called on the power of prayer. Throughout the book, Nehemiah sought refuge in the comforting arms of the God of heaven. Nehemiah's prayer moved the heart of God, changed the mind of a king, stirred up the passion, confidence, and determination of a people, rebuilt broken walls, and started social and spiritual revival in his homeland. Prayer will also be the spark that ignites revival and restoration in us and our homeland.

If you still doubt the power and necessity of prayer, study the prayer life of Jesus. Jesus, the earthly manifestation of the divine, relied on and modeled prayer. A day in the life of Christ shows us how it's done.

See Mark 1:35–45 for a day in the life of Jesus. What did Jesus do that day?

How did Jesus begin that day? (See Mark 1:35.)

What happened while He was praying? (See Mark 1:35–37.)

Jesus got up early in the morning to pray, but the demands of His life still intruded on His prayertime. Even Jesus had to carve out time for prayer! But Jesus knew that His life was ruled by His relationship with God. They needed to be in continual communion.

In what situations did Jesus make time to pray?

Luke 5:15–16

Luke 6:12

Luke 9:18

Luke 22:39–46

We live hectic lives. Americans are working longer hours and have less leisure time than ever. For many women, our workday continues into the night because of the demands of family and home.

The problem is magnified for African American women. Many Black women are the sole support of their families. Black married couples have less income compared with White married couples with similar educational backgrounds. Often husband and wife must both work to maintain their standard of living. Each of us must deal with the demands of being a Black woman in America. This is all the more reason, Black Christian women ought always to pray. What hinders you from spending more time in conversation with God?

GIVE IT UP

Nehemiah 1:4 tells us that when Nehemiah heard the news about his homeland, he mourned and fasted in addition to praying. He raised a few eyebrows when he refused to eat the fine, rich foods prepared by the palace chefs. People agreed that maybe he was taking this diet thing to the extreme. *The problem must be more serious than that*, they thought. He was spending more time by himself. He didn't talk as much or laugh as loudly as he did before the visitors from Jerusalem came. Nehemiah was plainly desperate for God's help and direction.

Women of God, there are some situations we face that require prayer and fasting. There are some places of bondage in our lives and the lives of those we love that cause us to cry out in bitter tears to God. We show our commitment by letting go of anything that is ahead of our relationship with God. When the bondage is deep, it takes prayer and fasting. Now, I mean fasting wisely and as our health permits—we aren't trying to harm ourselves.

What do I mean by fasting? I mean pushing back the fried chicken, collards, sweet potato pie, green beans, cake, or whatever your favorite is. I mean giving up television, radio, CDs, DVDs, or whatever entertainment you're addicted to. I mean by fasting that we take less time for ourselves and more time to connect to the Power Source of the universe. What Nehemiah did required discipline. Nehemiah's discipline led to his success in the palace. Discipline permeated his prayer life. The same discipline will strengthen our people and deepen our spiritual walk.

WAITING ON GOD

We are informed every day of some individual, community, or country in crisis. We don't know what we can do, and we don't know where to start. Problems among Blacks often leave us feeling helpless. Nehemiah's answer is that we start with prayer.

Quietly, Nehemiah began asking God to let him do something for Jerusalem. He searched in prayer for the next step he should take. Naturally, Nehemiah wanted to begin to address the problem immediately. But he stilled his heart and waited on consent and direction from God.

YOU HAVE BEEN MADE WORTHY

Did Nehemiah wonder if he was the right one for the job? Could God use him for something of such importance? Centuries before Nehemiah's birth, the Law of Moses declared that eunuchs were unworthy to enter the temple of God (Deuteronomy 23:1). Bible scholars disagree, but some think that Nehemiah was a eunuch. A eunuch is a castrated male. For this reason, eunuchs were given charge of the royal apartment where the queen resided. You may recall the problems a handsome Joseph had with the overly interested wife of his boss Potiphar (Genesis 39). Kings didn't want virile men around their womenfolk. You get the point I'm trying to make.

Later, however, the prophet Isaiah declared that God had thrown open the door of the temple and welcomed eunuchs into the sanctuary (Isaiah 56:1–8). So by Nehemiah's time, eunuchs were allowed to enter the temple and participate in worship. The temple in ancient times was considered the place where God resided. We all have had something that makes us unworthy of God's holy presence. The good news is that we have been made worthy to serve and worship God through faith in Jesus Christ. God is a God of inclusion—not exclusion (Galatians 3:23–29). God is not a respecter of persons. Say amen, somebody!

THE FULLNESS OF TIME

What God would do through Nehemiah would answer the prayers of past generations of Israelites. A hundred years earlier, Jeremiah had in the same breath prophesied Jerusalem's destruction and God's promised deliverance. Generations in exile had come and gone, countless prayers had been prayed for the restoration of Israel. Prophets like Ezekiel, Daniel, and Haggai called the nation to faithfulness and prayed for their return to their former glory. Nehemiah's prayers drew from the very phrases they used. We don't know when, we don't know where, and we don't know how, but my dears, we know our God answers prayers.

Nehemiah as yet did not fully understand that he was on the verge of bringing God's answer to Jerusalem. All he knew was that to fulfill his role in Jerusalem's urban revitalization program, he needed the approval of his boss, King Artaxerxes. He knew that God had to make it happen. Nehemiah used prayer to bypass the world's power and made his request to the almighty God of the universe.

NEHEMIAH'S MODEL PRAYER

Nehemiah's prayer expressed his confidence in the power of the "God of heaven" to rescue and to restore. He was desperate for God's deliverance, so he used the most powerful tool the Christian has—prayer. The prayer found in Nehemiah 1:4–11 shows us some essential ingredients to powerful, restoring prayer. Nehemiah did some things that are good for us to do too!

1. **He ran to the throne of God (Nehemiah 1:4).** Nehemiah ran to the throne of grace. No problem is too insignificant or too overwhelming for our compassionate and loving God to handle. He wants us to share our lives, hurts, temptations, anxieties, and frustrations with Him.

What does the Bible teach us about God's desire to hear from us?

Matthew 7:7–12

Luke 18:1–8

Yes, God urgently desires to hear from us. Everything we ask that is consistent with His will shall be granted to us. We should not fear entering the presence of God through prayer.

What will we find at the throne of God? (See Hebrews 4:16.)

Yes, we will find mercy and grace to help us in our time of need. In ancient Israel, spotless animals were offered as sacrifices in the temple, where the presence of God abided.

What sacrifice should we bring into God's presence?

Psalm 51:17

Romans 12:1−2

2. **He recalled the attributes of God (Nehemiah 1:5a).** Our prayers are placed in proper perspective when we recall the traits and character of the God we serve. Slaves in the midst of that most cruel of American institutions figured that their God was faithful and compassionate. They figured out through their experience that God loved them and hated slavery. Their God was a God of justice and liberation. Their God considered all humanity equal. Their God would someday break the bonds of slavery. They knew the character of God.

What have your experiences taught you about the nature and character of God?

What words did Nehemiah use to describe the nature of God? (See Nehemiah 1:5a.)

Nehemiah knew that God was great and awesome.

How do the following verses testify to the fact that God is great and awesome?

Psalm 19:1−4

Genesis 1:1−4

Romans 1:16−17

John 1:1−2

3. **He resounded the faithfulness of God (Nehemiah 1: 5b, 10).** Nehemiah praised God for what God had already done. God is the one who "keeps His covenant of love with those who love Him and obey His commands." The covenant was made because God loved Israel. God is faithful. God had proven His faithfulness to Israel throughout their history. God was faithful even when Israel was unfaithful. Certainly, we can say that God has been faithful to us even when, in rebellion, we have been unfaithful to Him. Our God is worthy of our praise. Praising God does at least three things:
   1. It gives to God the credit and praise due to the Creator and Sustainer of the universe;
   2. It brings joy to our spirits, minds and souls;
   3. It increases our faith that God who has delivered before will do it again. So begin your prayers by recalling who God is and what God has already done. Surely we agree with our forefathers and foremothers that God has brought us a mighty long way.

Share a time in your life when God proved His love and faithfulness to you. (See Hebrews 10:23.)

4. **He repented of unfaithfulness to God (Nehemiah 1:6–7).** Nehemiah acknowledged his own sin, his family's sin, and Israel's sin. Nehemiah asked forgiveness for the sinfulness of others. Rather than having no sympathy for Israel, he linked their plight to their failure to be faithful to the Sinai covenant. He repented for any known and unknown sins he or his family may have committed. Nehemiah recalled God's warning that if they were unfaithful to the Sinai covenant, they would be scattered.

If they repented of their sins, what had God promised to do? (See Deuteronomy 30:1–10.)

Nehemiah was straight up with God; they had been wrong and he knew it. The late Dr. Anthony Campbell, former professor of homiletics at Boston University, stated in a sermon illustration that there are three stages every Black man goes through when he has gotten himself in a tight situation. Stage 1: He's indignant—"You don't know that I . . ." Stage 2: He gets loud—"You don't know WHO I AM." Stage 3: He gets pitiful—"Baby, baby, p-l-e-a-s-e!" Not only Black men do that! This is the nature of human beings. We hate to admit that we are wrong. Of course the brothers are going to do it in their own unique way. But with God, it must be a straight up cry for mercy when we are wrong. When we ask God for forgiveness after genuine repentance, God will forgive! Repentance also includes a commitment to obedience.

What does Matthew 6:12–15 teach us about repentance?

5. **He relied on the promises of God (Nehemiah 1:8–9).** Israel was given every opportunity to repent before they were devastated by Babylon and carried into captivity. After their captivity, God kept the door open for them to return to Him. If and when they did, He promised them deliverance and restoration of their losses. War and bad things happen to good people. But Israel's predicament, the prophets explained, was linked to their sin. God consistently provided His patience, everlasting mercy, and love. Nehemiah relied on the Word of God. God's Word is true and never failing.

What does Paul say about the promises of God? (See 2 Corinthians 1:15–22.)

The promises of God to those who believe are countless.

Discover four of these promises of God to those who believe.

John 3:16

Mark 11:24

John 14:12

Matthew 6:31–33

Sister saints, as Elizabeth Ravenell of my parents' church family would say, "Who wouldn't serve a God like that?"

6. **He resorted to the mercy of God (Nehemiah 1:10–11a).** Nehemiah, knowing that his people were still away from God, relied on the mercy of God. The ninth chapter of Nehemiah lists the history of God's love for Israel. It tells of God's constant acts of grace and mercy.

God continuously showed His mercy. The old sisters of the church would say, "Have mercy, Lord." Have you every realized that you do not deserve some favor of God and had to cry out, "Lord, have mercy on me"? In the same way, Nehemiah pleaded and relied on the mercy of God. As Christians we have experienced God's grace and mercy. God shows mercy to the good, the bad, and the indifferent. And He wants us to learn to be like that too.

How should Christians behave toward those we feel do not deserve mercy? (See Matthew 5:43–48.)

We learn from Nehemiah that in our conversations with God we must:

- Recall the _____ of God (Nehemiah 1:5a).

- Resound the _____ of God (Nehemiah 1:5b, 10).

- Repent of any _____ to God (Nehemiah 1:6–7).

- Rely on the _____ of God (Nehemiah 1:8–9).

- Resort to the _____ of God (Nehemiah 1:10–11a).

But Nehemiah's prayer was not yet complete.

7. **He asked God to help him take the very next step (Nehemiah 1:11b).** Nehemiah's prayer had been dealing with the whole history of Israel, but it led up to this one specific moment: Nehemiah was about to go to his boss, the king, and ask for permission to go to Jerusalem to rebuild the wall. It was a long shot. King Artaxerxes had no special love of Israel or Jerusalem. Nehemiah was a trusted and valued

servant; the king liked having him around. The king also held Nehemiah's life in his hands. To make this request, Nehemiah needed all the courage God could give him, and he needed God to soften the king's heart. He was ready to take the next step.

We can pray all day long, but when we get off our knees we need to get ready to take the next step. God is going to have something for us to do. In Lesson Three, we'll see the next step God had in mind for Nehemiah.

Marian Wright Edelman has put "feet" to her prayers.

MARIAN WRIGHT EDELMAN

Marian Wright Edelman, a career-long advocate for the disadvantaged, was born June 6, 1939, in Bennettsville, South Carolina, youngest of Arthur Jerome Wright and Maggie Leola (Bowen) Wright's five children. By their own deeds, the Wrights instilled in their children a strong sense of service to others. A Baptist minister, Marian's father wrote, "Service is the rent we pay to be living. It is the very purpose of life and not something you do in your spare time."

Marian was expected to help with chores at the nearby Wright Home for the Aged, the first such institution for African Americans in South Carolina, founded by her father and managed by her mother.

Marian attended Spelman College, and later on scholarship at Yale Law, due to her desire to help others and contribute to social progress. She later explained she wanted "to be able to help black people, and the law seemed like a tool [I] needed."

As a lawyer for the NAACP, after moving to Jackson, Mississippi, to continue her work to direct the NAACP Legal Defense and Educational Fund office, Marian became the first African American woman to pass Mississippi's bar exam. After lobbying successfully for the restoration of federal funds for the Mississippi Head Start programs, Marian's subsequent lifelong effort: to lobby for children's interests.

A career move in 1968 to Washington, D.C., to serve as counsel for the Poor People's Campaign organized by Dr. Martin Luther King Jr., also brought marriage to Peter Edelman, a former assistant to Robert F. Kennedy. In D.C., she founded the Washington Research Project, a public-interest law firm that is parent organization for the Children's Defense Fund Wight Edelman established in 1973. Through this venue, Marian continued her advocacy: to persuade Congress to overhaul views and legislation concerning handicapped, homeless, abused and neglected children. "If you don't like the way the world is, you have an obligation to change it. Just do it one step at a time," Were her beliefs, words, and actions.

Edelman lobbied diligently for **fully-funded Head Start, proper medical insurance for all children and their pregnant mothers, vaccinations for every child, and an expanded children's tax credit** for children. All built on her foundational belief:

> "Investing in [children] is not a national luxury or a national choice. It's a national necessity. If the foundation of your house is crumbling, you don't say you can't afford to fix it while you're building astronomically expensive fences to protect it from outside enemies. The issue is not are we going to pay—it's are we going to pay now, upfront, or are we going to pay a whole lot more later on."

Marian Wright Edelman's books include *Guide My Feet: Prayers and Meditations on Loving and Working for Children,* in which she writes that the crises children face are due to the actions and inactions of many human beings. These crises, she writes, can be overcome by many human taking actions overtime, and with God's help.

As the title of Wright Edelman's book demonstrate and her actions as a caretaker to generations demonstrates, through prayer, we have the power of God's restoration in our lives and can have an impact on others' for God's good.

LESSON SUMMATION

My sisters, we will not be restored until we get desperate for the ways of God. We must become desperate enough to let go of anything that comes ahead of or instead of communion with God. God is leaning over the balcony listening for our prayers—ready, willing, and able to rescue and revive us again. When we pray with faith, sincerity, and consistency, the power of God will flow in us and through us. We will speed up the time when God will rule in us and reign on earth as He does in heaven.

Commit today to regular daily times of prayer. If there is a spiritual stronghold in your life, lay aside every weight that is holding you back. Lay your life, marriage, children, job, ministry, community, and nation on the altar. When you do this and patiently wait, God will send His ministering Spirit to whisper His love and instructions in your ear. Your task may be in your home, at school, at church, on the job, or in your neighborhood. God is waiting in heaven with the directions and power to accomplish it.

ᴅDAILYᴅDEVOTIONS

LESSON TWO
LORD, TEACH US TO PRAY

The supreme model for our prayer life is Jesus Christ. His example sparked this question from the disciples, His closest earthly companions: "Lord, teach us how to pray" (Luke 11:1–4). The prayer that Christ shared with them is a model prayer. A longer version of the Lord's Prayer is found in Matthew 6:9–15. To strengthen your prayer life, spend time in prayer this week focusing on the elements of the Lord's Prayer.

DAY ONE

"Our Father in heaven, hallowed be your name" (Matthew 6:9). Almighty God, who rules from heaven, is also the One the old spirituals called, "a father for the fatherless and a mother for the motherless." This Father requires obedience. Where we go and how we behave reflect on the family name. His resources are available upon our asking, and we will ultimately inherit the riches of heaven. But our heavenly Father's love and power exceed that of our earthly parents. Let this knowledge encourage you as you go to God in prayer.

Hallowed means holy, apart from the commonplace or the wicked. We pray that the holiness of God will be recognized, acknowledged, and worshipped throughout the earth.

Put this prayer request in your own words.

DAY TWO

"Your kingdom come, your will be done on earth as it is in heaven" (Matthew 6:10). This petition is that the reign of God will be manifested on earth in the same way it is in heaven. The kingdom of God is already present in the hearts of those who believe in God through Jesus Christ. His presence in our hearts is evidenced by our obedience to His two greatest commandments: loving God first and foremost and loving our neighbors as we love ourselves. Daily, we must pray for the coming of the kingdom—the sovereignty or dominion— of God in the hearts of all people.

Put this prayer request in your own words.

DAY THREE

"Give us today our daily bread" (Matthew 6:11). This petition is for the daily necessities of life. The admonition of Christ is that we put our lives in order by seeking first the kingdom of God and His righteousness (Matthew 6:33). Following the guidance of God through His Word and Holy Spirit, requests for our daily provisions are to be offered to God. God will abundantly provide for us according to His riches in glory.

With this knowledge, how should you handle any anxieties about the future?

DAY FOUR

"Forgive us our debts, as we also have forgiven our debtors"
(Matthew 6:12). This petition recognizes that we will and do
sin—miss the mark of God. This clearly states that we will receive
forgiveness from God in the same measure we grant forgiveness
to others. Jesus brings this point home and places it on the living
room table in Matthew 6:14–15. Invite God to give you a forgiving
heart. Ask God to help you forgive recent or past, small or deep
transgressions against you.

Remind yourself how many times God has forgiven you. Put that prayer request
in your own words.

DAY FIVE

"And lead us not into temptation, but deliver us from the evil one"
(Matthew 6:13). Temptation is some kind of bait or lure to do evil.
This prayer asks God to keep us from committing a deliberate act of
evil against God or our neighbor. Another way to state the first part
of the verse is, "Do not let us give in to temptation." Additionally, the
verse could mean, "Help us overcome tests of our faith." Abraham
was tested by God to determine if he would sacrifice his son Isaac.
Each temptation escaped or test passed makes us stronger in faith
and proves our loyalty to God.

Put this petition in your own words.

"For yours is the kingdom and the power and the glory forever. Amen." This closing doxology or benediction to the Lord's Prayer is not found in the oldest manuscripts of this Gospel. Your Bible may not have it, or may have it as a footnote. This closing moves us back to the source of our strength and lives—God. It is a praise song to end the time of communion with our awesome God. Close today with a song of praise that acknowledges the greatness of God.

WAITING WITH FAITH

NEHEMIAH 2:1–9

VITAL VERSES

"The king said to me, 'What is it you want?' Then I prayed to the God of heaven, and I answered the king, 'If it pleases the king and if your servant has found favor in his sight, let him send me to the city in Judah where my fathers are buried so that I can rebuild it.'. . . And because the gracious hand of my God was upon me, the king granted my requests."

— NEHEMIAH 2:4–5, 8

KEY TERMS

Faith: Nehemiah took a leap of faith based on his knowledge of God's previous faithfulness. Nehemiah trusted because God had been absolutely reliable throughout his life. Faith is more than saying we trust, it is acting on God's trustworthiness even when the outcome is uncertain or unseen (Romans 3:3; Hebrews 11:1). Faith without accompanying works of righteousness is not faith at all (James 2:11–26). By faith we receive salvation through Jesus Christ.

Grace: Mercy and favor. God gave grace to Nehemiah and the people of Judah when He softened the heart of the king, who showed favor to Nehemiah. This favor was a direct answer to Nehemiah's prayer (Nehemiah 1:11). God's greatest expression of grace/graciousness was salvation through Jesus Christ (Romans 5:1–2).

Hand of God: Symbol of God's sovereignty. God alone reigns over the universe and those who dwell therein. God is not just powerful, God is the source of all power. God's right hand gives strength, authority, the Holy Spirit, and blessings (Acts 11:21).

Nisan: In the calendar of Nehemiah's time, Nisan is a month that comes in the spring around March or April (Nehemiah 2:1).

African American women know about waiting. We have waited for our freedom, waited for our men to come home, waited for our children to grow up, and waited for justice to come.

During times of waiting, God wants us to wait with faith, believing that His work is going on even when we can't see it. Waiting with faith doesn't mean that we do nothing—we keep on working and praying and doing the jobs that the Lord has left for us to do. But sometimes we see a mountain we just can't cross or a tree we can't uproot, and we can't figure out what to do next. In those times, we have to let our faith in God keep us from despair.

That time of waiting might be the time when God is raising up someone—maybe even you—who will move that mountain or uproot that tree. Time and time again, God has done this. To proceed in our mission of restoration, we must be women of faith. With faith the size of a mustard seed, we can conquer every obstacle and move every mountain. Lord, increase our faith! (See Luke 17:5–6.)

- By faith, an unnamed woman with an issue of blood, risking shame and rejection, pressed through the crowd, touched the hem of the Savior's garment, and was made whole (Luke 8:42b–48).

- By faith, an unnamed Canaanite woman pleaded, begged, and refused to take no for an answer. Her great confidence in the power of God was noted by the Master, and her daughter was healed (Matthew 15:22–28).

- Mary McLeod Bethune moved mountains when, with one dollar and some change, she founded, built up, and provided leadership for Bethune-Cookman College. She moved mountains when she founded a national women's organization, the National Council of Negro Women, and later served on the "Black Cabinet" (Federal Council on Negro Affairs) of President Franklin D. Roosevelt.

- By faith, Mary accepted her call, though a virgin, to mother the Savior of the world. In shock and confusion, she wept as He freely gave His life on Calvary's cross. With the faith of a humble servant, she waited for the outpouring of the Holy Spirit and became a founding member of the first church of Jerusalem and the world (Acts 1:12–14).

- By faith, Deborah ignited hope in Barak's heart; she co-led the outnumbered and poorly equipped Israelite army in battle against the superior forces of the Canaanites. God fought the battle and gained the victory, and their people lived in peace for 40 years (Judges 4–5).

- Nannie Helen Burroughs uprooted the trees of the status quo in her speech to the 1900 National Baptist Convention entitled, "How the Sisters Are Hindered from Helping." This speech led to the birth of the Women's Convention, an auxiliary of the National Baptist Convention, that today numbers in the tens of thousands and supports the mission of God in the world.

Space does not permit us to tell of Harriet Tubman, Rahab, Rosa Parks, Lydia, Sojourner Truth, Abigail, Frances Harper, Hagar, Esther, Hannah, and countless others whose faith uprooted trees of fear and moved mountains of doubt and despair. These trees and mountains held back the destiny of an idea, a person, a nation, or a people. It takes faith to move such things, so Lord, increase our faith! It does not take much more than we already have—it just takes faith the size of a mustard seed. You and I have that much, and we shouldn't let the forces of the evil one convince us otherwise.

Lord, increase our faith!

IN THE MEANTIME

Have you heard it said that God answers our prayers in three ways—*yes*, *no*, and *wait*? Sometimes *wait* can be the hardest answer to take. It takes faith to wait patiently. Nehemiah waited patiently on God. It had been three months since his brother Hanani's visit, since he had learned of Jerusalem's destruction, since he prayed for an opportunity to ask his boss, the king of Persia, for help. Winter turned to spring and Nehemiah still waited for God to reveal the answer to his prayer. He put his hope in the promises of God.

We must increase our confidence in the faithfulness of God. Have faith that whether God's answers take milliseconds, minutes, hours, days, months, years—that God answers prayers. As old folk have said, God "may not come when you want Him, but He's always on time." Waiting is not just a good idea; waiting is commanded.

What do the following verses teach us about waiting on God?

Isaiah 40:28–31

Matthew 25:1–13

Romans 8:19

What should we do while waiting for the Lord? Often our waiting period is a time of preparation. God may be preparing us, others, and the situation. Before Hanani and the Israelite delegation conceived in their minds to visit Susa, God was preparing Nehemiah for it. In the months after Hanani's visit, God planted in Nehemiah's mind a blueprint for the renewal of Jerusalem. God prepared the heart of King Artaxerxes to be open to Nehemiah's proposal. Nehemiah did his homework, finding out the resources needed to rebuild the walls and gates. When the day came for Nehemiah's leap of faith, he had his act together.

Take time now to read this week's main Scripture, Nehemiah 2:1–9.

On the day that Nehemiah took his leap of faith, he saw the greatness and graciousness of God. Of course, he knew that his actions could result in his death. Persian kings were bad that way—you could tick them off by showing up to work in a bad mood. Bad moods and the wrong request could get a guy capital punishment. Despite those who would have advised Nehemiah to do otherwise, on that spring day, God told Nehemiah to take the leap of faith.

Why did Nehemiah do it? Nehemiah loved God, his people, and his homeland, but he had other options. Nehemiah could have copped an attitude and said, "I got mine (success); they (Israel) got theirs to get." He could have eased his conscience with a sizeable charitable contribution. He could have felt or done nothing at all. But when God says go (and make sure that God is the One sending you), I recommend absolute obedience. God can make life uncomfortable here—ask anybody who has rejected a clear calling from God. Never forget that God determines our eternal destiny.

FAITH AND SMARTS: NEHEMIAH 2:1−2

My mom used to say when her girls did something smart, "So you're using your head for more than a hat rack." Nehemiah used his head when he appealed to King Artaxerxes. He knew he had a huge favor to ask from the king. He had taken time to figure the requirements of his restoration and revitalization program. He was ready to act.

On the first day of the new year, which fell in the month of Nisan, any request made to the king would be granted. According to the historian Herodotus, it was customary for the Persian king to show favor at this feast each year. The law of the feast required that no one at the king's table that day who asked a boon (benefit, blessing) should be denied his request. Surely Nehemiah thought of this custom as he planned when he would approach his boss. Nehemiah used his head for more than a hat rack. Yet he was risking his life all the same. The king could decide that he wanted one less Jewish cupbearer on his piece of the universe.

On that day, Nehemiah let down his guard. He had been carrying on with his work, waiting for the right time to act, but behaving as if everything were normal. Now, he stopped pretending that everything was wonderful. He dropped the mask.

Wine was being served, and it was probably a banquet. The king received the wine from the hands of his servant, God's servant, Nehemiah. The king noticed that Nehemiah's appearance was as neat and polished as ever, but something was different. So King Artaxerxes inquired with genuine concern and discernment, "Why does your face look so sad when you are not ill? This can be nothing but sadness of heart" (v. 2). This was obviously grief—he was depressed. Unaware of the unseen hand of God, King Artaxerxes was simply concerned about his favored cupbearer. You see, God has the heart of the king in His hands. Consider Proverbs 21:1: "The king's heart is in the hand of the Lord; he directs it like a watercourse wherever He pleases." God does that with whomever He pleases, whenever He pleases.

KEEP ON PRAYING: NEHEMIAH 2:3–4

In telling the story, Nehemiah admitted that he was scared stiff at this point. But Nehemiah was a wise man. He showed the king proper respect. He shared his situation in language that would touch the king's heart. Nehemiah knew that Persians had great regard for their ancestors and invested in their graves. King Artaxerxes was at the time preparing his own elaborate burial place. So Nehemiah carefully weighed his words and responded, "May the king live forever! Why should my face not look sad when the city where my fathers are buried lies in ruins, and its gates have been destroyed by fire?" The king then asked the question that opened the door to Nehemiah's prayers being answered: "What is it you want?"

Before answering, Nehemiah silently, quickly, and quietly entered the throne room of God without leaving the presence of the king. He said a split-second prayer, crying out for the wisdom and intervention of God. Once again, we see that Nehemiah was a man of prayer. Prayer blanketed his life. His success was in God's hands.

LORD GIVE ME THE WORDS: NEHEMIAH 2:4b–6

Nehemiah prayed for God to give him the right words: "Show me, Lord, how to put it." God's insight helped Nehemiah formulate his reply (Matthew 10:17–20; Luke 21:15). He kept his Holy Spirit–empowered cool. He remembered that the king had no love for the city of Jerusalem, so he did not specifically mention it in his response. Nehemiah wanted the king to remember he had been no slacker in his task as cupbearer. So Nehemiah said, "If it pleases the king and if your servant has found favor in his sight, let him send me to the city in Judah where my fathers are buried so that I can rebuild it."

The queen, Damaspia, was present, and Nehemiah noted her presence. Did she speak up for or against Nehemiah's proposal, or did she remain silent? Often the spouses of persons in power have great influence (see Esther). Many commentators hold that Nehemiah was a personal favorite of the Queen and that she spoke up for him at this moment. If she did, thank you, Queen Damaspia, for showing us how the right word at the right time can change history!

The king considered his response. King Artaxerxes knew that the residents of Jerusalem had a history of rebelling against their rulers. God, however, showed Artaxerxes how this program could help him quell the rising military instability among the other nations in that area of his territory. That very time might be a good time to rebuild the walls and gates of Jerusalem to protect that region. Nehemiah had been a faithful servant and trustworthy advisor and was looking like the ideal person to be the governor of Judah.

The king signaled his intent to grant Nehemiah's request: "How long will your journey take, and when will you get back?" Nehemiah had a ready reply and gave the king a time frame. Nehemiah's request was granted! This decision gave Nehemiah the right to rule the area on the king's behalf. We discover later in this story that he did, in fact, become the governor of Judah (Nehemiah 5:14, 18).

Girlfriends, we *have not* because we fail to ask God for it; when we ask God earnestly in faith, according to His will, God will grant our requests (James 5:13–18).

Nehemiah did not start into his full shout of praise until his task was completed. He had studied the situation and determined the necessities of his journey and the material requirements of the enterprise. He knew that he would need more than a leave of absence. He would need military protection as he traveled in hostile territory. He needed a reference letter with the king's seal, stating that the king approved what he was doing. He needed timber and supplies to rebuild the gates and walls. He needed a place to stay when he reached Jerusalem. Convinced that God's hand was upon him, Nehemiah told the king his needs. The king granted Nehemiah all of his requests.

THE HAND OF GOD: NEHEMIAH 2:8–9

Some of us might have left the room and bragged about how we outwitted the king. But Nehemiah refused the credit. He thanked the king and left the room shouting praises to the God of heaven, ruler of the universe. He knew that he succeeded because "the gracious hand of God" was upon him. The hand of God represents God's sovereign power—His supreme rule. God's hand empowers those who trust Him. God directed every aspect of this encounter with the king. Nehemiah recognized that what happened was a "God thing."

Nehemiah took his credentials to the governors of the Trans-Euphrates. The king's letters of recommendation permitted him to begin his long journey to his homeland. He had the necessary military escort, which included army officers and cavalry of Persia. As he traveled, surely he was listening as God brought His final plans together in Nehemiah's mind. Surely he was on a spiritual high. God again proved that He is faithful and truthful. Nehemiah smiled, laughed, and sang as he was strengthened by the joy he had in the Lord. His escorts probably asked him why he was smiling to himself. He only smiled more and talked about the goodness of God.

WORKING IT OUT

During his leap of faith, Nehemiah took a moment to shoot a prayer upward to God.

The Bible notes several arrow (short and to the point) prayers. What were some of these prayers as found in the following Scriptures?

Moses at the Red Sea (Exodus 14:13–15)

The Disciples in the Storm (Matthew 8:25)

Peter Sinking in the Sea (Matthew 14:30)

Nehemiah realized that God's hand was on his life.

What recent events have convinced you of the presence of God's hand on your life?

It's sometimes easier to see God's hand working in extraordinary or difficult events. It is important that we be alert to the hand of God in both the large and the small miracles of our lives.

How do you see God's hand of favor working in your life and the life of those you love?

DROP THE MASK

Nehemiah had to drop the mask he wore in order to do God's will. The king was used to seeing Nehemiah in good spirits, but Nehemiah had to reveal his grief and longing in order to achieve his purpose. He had to drop his mask.

While I was in high school, my sister Teresa brought home from college a book of poetry called *Black Voices*. I read it with fascination because so many of the gifted Black poets truly voiced the yearnings, heartbreaks, and joy of my people. One poem, "We Wear the Mask," was written by Paul Laurence Dunbar. The poem was written more than one hundred years ago, but its words still relate in some ways to the circumstances of Black folk today. All humans, in one way or another, at some time or another, have worn or attempted to wear masks. Here's the poem:

We Wear the Mask

We wear the mask that grins and lies,
It hides our cheeks and shades our eyes, —
This debt we pay to human guile;
With torn and bleeding hearts we smile,
And mouth with myriad subtleties.

Why should the world be overwise,'
In counting all our tears and sighs?
Nay, let them only see us, while
We wear the mask.

We smile, but, O great Christ, our cries
To thee from tortured souls arise.
We sing, but oh the clay is vile
Beneath our feet, and long the mile;
But let the world dream otherwise,
We wear the mask!

—Paul Laurence Dunbar

As persons of faith, we should be totally transparent with our precious Lord. In fact, God rejects our attempts to pretend and yearns for our sincerity. God knows our thoughts before we can form and speak them. In prayer, the Holy Spirit communicates in groanings that cannot be spoken. God knew us before we knew ourselves—God knit us together in our mother's womb.

That is a powerful thing for a struggling Christian African American woman to know—that God knows. It makes my heart leap. The good news is that God knows all about you and me—our past, present, and future—and still loves us. Consider how God is always there, always knowing and caring, by reviewing Psalm 139.

Write a prayer of praise that God knows us and will share His thoughts with us.

COMPANIONS FOR OUR FAITH JOURNEY

The king gave Nehemiah companions (a military escort) for his journey to Jerusalem.

Identify some of the companions on our faith journey.

Companions that "have our back covered," as they follow us (Psalm 23:6):

A companion who is always with us (Matthew 28:20):

A companion who comforts, counsels, guides, and speaks the truth (John 16:5−15):

A companion closer than a blood relative (Proverbs 18:24):

Yes, if we go where God leads, we have companionship for the journey. Every Christian can rejoice in this knowledge. More than 50 percent of Black women are single by design, choice, or circumstance. As women of God, we are never alone.

Nehemiah's every need for this project was met. God will provide for all our needs if we seek first His guidance.

See Philippians 4:4−9. What should we be anxious about?

What should we do instead?

IDONG EKANDEM HAS HAD FAITH TO MOVE MOUNTAINS.

Idong is wife to Bennett Ekandem, director of the Family Heritage Foundation (FHF), and their three sons. This Christian servant labors alongside Bennett as they minister to children at-risk, underprivileged children, and refugee families. Through FHF, they offer afterschool programs, summer programs, computer training, youth development program, and microenterprise training. Their mission is to help children and their families by providing enrichment and outreach programs that meet their needs.

> "Every child is a gift to our community," FHF writes. "He or she is tomorrow's leader, the hope for our future, the strength and pillar of our nation. Every child deserves a safe haven, with responsive, loving care and opportunities that develop character and provide social equality. We believe it is essential to provide the fundamental needs of families in order for children to become successful. These families have a need for spiritual, social, physical, and intellectual development. We also believe that a safe community produces a healthy family.
>
> "In Family Heritage Foundation, we have a vision for safer communities, stronger families, and responsible youth. We work hard to ensure that our youth and their families have access to educational and enrichment programs.
>
> "Consequently, these developed youth and families can work together to develop their communities and make them safer. As a result of more opportunities for social equality, crime rates and penury levels will drop significantly."

Idong writes about her own childhood and the obstacles to her faith development, "I gave my life to Jesus Christ at the age of 16, in Nigeria. As the only Christian in my family, I faced persecution from my parents and other relatives. However, this persecution only made my faith stronger and drove me to pray for my family's salvation. My dad eventually gave his life to Christ and then the rest of my family became born again. After a few years, I began to drift from God but I always knew He loved me. At 26, I married Bennett and moved to the United States. We got married in 1998 and I finally settled in America a year later.

"As time went by, I realized that I had not been pursuing an *authentic* relationship with Jesus. I knew I was saved, but I was more focused on doing the "right" thing than having that intimate relationship with my Savior. I served alongside Bennett's mission to refugees in Clarkston, Georgia. I was faithful in service, but I still felt a vacuum that missions work could not fill.

"After a ten year battle with endometriosis and infertility, I became broken and totally surrendered to Jesus. That was when I began to desire Him more than anything else in the world. Two years later, God blessed my husband and me with three beautiful boys through adoption.

"We adopted Samuel, Jeremiah, and Caleb (biological brothers) on the same day. God answered my prayers and granted my heart's desire to be a godly mother! He restored my joy.

"Life as a missionary and adoptive mother to three boys has had its joy and challenges. Yet, in all my trials and difficulties, God has always shown Himself faithful and strong. He guides me by giving me clear instructions in His Word. He provides me with daily strength to balance the demands of ministry with my responsibilities in the home. He has enabled me to bond with my three sons and to help them with their own journey to healing from neglect and deprivation.

He anoints me to minister to women and young girls, leading them to Jesus, the One who restores their hope. I know that God is not done with me yet. He indeed causes all things to work together for good in my life (Romans 8:28)."

What an encouragement of God's faithfulness and our faith in Him.

LESSON SUMMATION

Nehemiah with faith trusted God to move the mountains and uproot the trees that held back the restoration of his people and homeland. His faith was tried and refined as he waited patiently for the God of heaven to answer his sincere prayers. God was preparing Nehemiah, the king, and the situation to bring His divine will to pass. Nehemiah trusted while he waited because God had been, is, and will be faithful to His people.

Nehemiah leaped in faith and landed in the mighty and loving arms of God. He prayed in faith as if everything depended on God. He researched and prepared as if everything depended on him. He gave credit to the true decision maker—God.

God touched the heart and changed the mind of a pagan king. He supplied Nehemiah beyond his wildest imagination. If you have tried before without success, try again. Listen for God's heart; read God's Word; obey God's voice. If we step and even leap out on the promises of God, God will catch us. Take a faith leap, and through God you'll move mountains and uproot trees.

It takes faith the size of a mustard seed. I have that much. How about you?

⚞Daily Devotions

LESSON THREE
MAKING THE LEAP OF FAITH

Nehemiah's faith is beginning to do the impossible. As God worked in the life of Nehemiah, He will work in your life. God will do far more than we ask, think, or imagine, through faith according the power that is at work in us. Let these Old and New Testament Scriptures enliven your study of Old Testament Nehemiah.

DAY ONE
Daily we should **meditate on the Word of God.**

What does Romans 10:17 teach us about the power of the Scripture? Spend some time today meditating on Isaiah 40:28–31.

DAY TWO
Rehearse daily the faithfulness of God. Time and again God has been faithful to us. God is in love with us and is faithful.

How should we respond to God's faithfulness? (See Lamentations 3:21–24; Philippians 4:8–9.)

DAY THREE

God, like a loving parent, gives us every good and perfect gift. We should **ask to increase our faith.**

Why is God the best place to go for more faith? (See Luke 18:8.)

DAY FOUR

Confess faith. Popular authors have spoken often of the power of the words we speak. If we speak faith, we will more often live faithfully. A Scripture that helps many people is Philippians 4:13.

Write this passage in your own words or write another verse of Scripture that encourages your faith.

DAY FIVE

Hang around people of faith. Ruth's association with Naomi resulted in her leaving the land and faith of her people and finding new life in God (Ruth 1:16). Barak was encouraged to go into battle because of the strong faith of Deborah (Judges 4:8). People who doubt your potential in God should be avoided.

How can believers help each other increase their faith? (See Colossians 3:15–17.)

LESSON FOUR

CALLED TO UNITY

NEHEMIAH 2:9 TO 3:32

VITAL VERSE

"I also told them about the gracious hand of my God upon me and what the king had said to me. They replied, 'Let us start rebuilding.' So they began this good work." —NEHEMIAH 2:18

KEY TERMS

Unity: In the Old Testament, *unity* is used in the sense of the togetherness of persons (Psalm 133:1), fellowship and praise (Psalm 34:3). In the New Testament, *unity* is used to refer to the oneness in faith that draws together the people of God (Ephesians 4:13).

Welfare: Prosperity, well-being, or interest (Nehemiah 2:10).

W hy can't we all just get along?" Just look at us, a people brought to this country in chains, who suffered hundreds of years of slavery and the horrors of racism. God is making it known to the world that we are civilization's comeback kids! God has blessed the African American community with loyal and capable educators, religious leaders, social workers, lawyers, engineers, healthcare professionals, general laborers, and others who daily try to apply God's standards—showing love to God, toward one another, and serving humanity. God's love has sustained us throughout our history, but some of us still find it hard to "just get along." Why?

Most of us would agree that the cruel hand of racism reaches out often to touch our daily lives. Yet we would be lying if we did not admit that our lack of unity also hinders us from achieving our divinely appointed goals and desires. Lack of unity robs us of the self-love and self-esteem necessary for inward peace and personal satisfaction. It strips us of the might to love one another and give witness to God's power to transform lives and rise above hate. I join with Susan L. Taylor, editor in chief of *Essence* magazine, in saying that we are our own greatest obstacles to liberation. Listen to her words from the book *How to Make Black America Better*:

> A strong and errant group is standing in the way of Black progress, and it is us. The central problem for African Americans—and for Black people throughout the world—is unity. This has been our problem historically. Today there is still little sense of kinship among the different tribes of African peoples. . . . We are each other's keeper. Everything and everyone on God's good earth is interconnected and has to be thought of as a whole. All that exists coexists. This is the simple yet difficult lesson the Creator has been trying to teach humanity—and First People, Black people—for eons. Love thy neighbor as thyself, for all of us together belong to a harmony, a community that is dependent, interdependent, on love.

Amen, Sister Susan. So let's go to this week's lesson, where Nehemiah motivates his people to unite in love to rebuild their land. His example will give us pointers in how we can be unified to rebuild and restore.

Take time now to read this week's main Scripture, Nehemiah 2:9 to 3:32.

Nehemiah's mission was to unify the people under the common goal of restoring the walls and gates of Jerusalem. Before his mission was completed, as the next three lessons will show, it seemed as if everyone and everything rebelled against his divinely given calling to do just that. But each lesson also shows Nehemiah's love for his land and people, and his fierce conviction that God would do what He said he would do.

As quickly as time would permit, Nehemiah had packed his bags and moved out of Susa, passport (king's letters) in hand. He reached his destination safely—after all, a military escort surrounded him. Nehemiah and his entourage would have traveled about 8 or 9 miles per day, so his approximately 900-mile trip home would have taken about 3 to 4 months. The length of the trip would have caused many of us to forego the trip and send a check instead! Nehemiah steeled his mind, quieted his heart, and calmed his spirit with the knowledge that he was doing the will of God.

EXPECT OPPOSITION: NEHEMIAH 2:9-10

When he arrived in Jerusalem, Nehemiah must have wondered, *where's the party?* Someone should have planned a welcome home party. A royal cupbearer, a man of wealth and status representing the interests of Persia, was coming to advance the wellbeing of Jerusalem. He would be its leading citizen—its governor. His counterpart governor, Sanballat of Samaria, and Tobiah, a leading Ammonite official, should have been ready to embrace and welcome him. Nehemiah had his fine recommendation letter from King Artaxerxes. With Persian military officers and cavalry members as escorts, Nehemiah merited some respect and recognition.

Instead, Sanballat and Tobiah were ticked off. They took the low (down) road, not the high (way to heaven) road. They took a path that human nature chooses far too many times, one crowded with folk willing to compromise human decency to keep others from prosperity. There are folk, and you have met some of them, who are not satisfied with keeping up with the Joneses; they want to climb the ladder of success using the backs of the Joneses as rungs on their way up. Sanballat and Tobiah were upset that someone was coming to help the economically struggling and spiritually depressed people of Jerusalem. They should have been ashamed, but we will discover as the story proceeds that these guys knew no shame. But if you have been in this world very long, you know that any great work for God stirs up opposition.

KEEP YOUR BALANCE: NEHEMIAH 2:11

Nehemiah knew to "pause for the cause" of his personal well-being. He accepted no social invitations, held no meetings, and made no decisions until he had had time to recover from his trip. He knew that the days ahead would require all of his physical, emotional, intellectual, and spiritual strength. So he wisely practiced what Christ's life modeled, pulling away *from* the heat of ministry to recover needed energy *for* that ministry.

COUNT THE COST: NEHEMIAH 2:12–16

After his recovery time, Nehemiah, using the moonlight, took a fact-gathering tour of the walls and gates of the city. At one point, he had to turn around because of the amount of charred rubble. His previous plans were based on his best estimate from what he heard from others. His servants walked as he alone rode on a beast of burden—one animal would not arouse the suspicion of inquiring minds. His heart was surely broken as he saw the devastated city, and tears likely fell, leaving traces on his face.

PROJECT THE VISION: NEHEMIAH 2:17-18

Nehemiah had to convince his people of the greatness and power of God and the possibility of restoration; it was time for Nehemiah to deliver the speech of his life. We have no proof of his giftedness as a speaker. He, like Paul, relied on the Holy Spirit. Only the outline is left of his four-point layperson's sermon. It was and is a powerful, spirit-lifting, bondage-breaking, mind-liberating message:

- "You see the trouble we are in: Jerusalem lies in ruins, and its gates have been burned" (Nehemiah 2:17). Nehemiah began with a realistic look at where they were. Positive change begins with dissatisfaction with the present circumstances, the status quo. Notice that Nehemiah did not point the finger. He personally identified with the plight of the people using the "we" when stating their trouble.

- "Come, let us rebuild the wall of Jerusalem, and we will no longer be in disgrace" (Nehemiah 2:17). *Nehemiah projected a vision.* As he built up the people's courage, self-esteem, and purpose, their passion was ignited. They decided to set aside personal aspirations for the good of the city, so all would be blessed.

- "I also told them about the gracious hand of my God upon me" (Nehemiah 2:18). He gave his *personal testimony of God's deliverance and provision.* In the recent past, he had seen the gracious hand of God at work (Nehemiah 2:8). Likewise, God's hand would be gracious toward them.

- "I also told them . . . what the king had said to me" (Nehemiah 2:18). The government had agreed to back the project. *Every obstacle* to the enterprise *had been cut down to size by the merciful hand of God.* God will do the same for us in family, church, community, nation, and world. In other words, we lost our way, the enemy tried to block us, but God makes a way out of no way.

Nehemiah poured out his heart, and the Spirit of God was in that place. If this were a church meeting in our community, some sister would start with a song like, "I Don't Feel Noways Tired." The congregation would form a long line to sign up for work crews. The response of Nehemiah's community was, "Let us start rebuilding" (Nehemiah 2:18). So they started the great work.

KEEP THE FAITH: NEHEMIAH 2:19–20

It seemed that before the benediction was finished, word got back to Sanballat and Tobiah. Geshem, the leader of the Arabs, joined them in their response. They poked fun at the Jews. They implied that the Israelites wanted to rebuild the walls to launch an attempt to overthrow their Persian rulers. In the past, the Samaritans had tried to block Jerusalem revitalization efforts (Ezra 4). Nehemiah responded that they were God's servants, that the work would go forward, and that they (Sanballat, Tobiah, and Geshem) had no right to be concerned about what God would do through the Israelites.

LEAVE YOUR LEGACY: NEHEMIAH 3:1–32

Nehemiah chapter 3 is a memorial to what happens when the people of God come together, focused on a common vision and united in purpose, and partner with God to rebuild. Like plaques in buildings, this chapter reminds us of those who came together for the common good of all Israel. We leave our legacy by what we do to touch and impact, for good or evil, the lives of others.

LET YOUR MOTIVE BE LOVE

Nehemiah immediately came upon opposition to the work he proposed. Every time the seed of a great work breaks through the soil, someone tries to pluck it out. When opposition comes, we must ensure that our motives line up with the will of God for us, and that what we are doing pleases God.

Has God put something in your heart to do? Consider this checklist. Will it line up with these things?
- ❏ The Word of God (Psalm 119:105; John 1:14)
- ❏ The life and teaching of Christ (1 Corinthians 10:31)
- ❏ The indwelling presence of the Holy Spirit (Romans 9:1)
- ❏ Wise and godly counsel (Colossians 3:16)
- ❏ Glorifying God (Matthew 5:13–16)
- ❏ Not causing others to stumble (Romans 14:21)
- ❏ Building up the body of Christ (Ephesians 4:15–16)
- ❏ Not tarnishing our temple (1 Corinthians 6:19–20)
- ❏ Not resulting in bondage to sin (1 Corinthians 6:12)
- ❏ Exemplifying love (1 Corinthians 13:1–3)

The bottom line is whether our actions are motivated by Christian love, what the Greeks defined as *agape* love. The greatest example of *agape* is God's gift of Jesus and Jesus' sacrifice of His life. In human terms, *agape* means selfless and self-giving love. This love is not be confused with *eros* (sexual love) or *philos* (friendship). The supreme description of God is that God is love. How do we live out this characteristic from our divine gene pool? It flows from our gratitude for the grace and love of God.

TOO STRESSED TO BE BLESSED?

Women often become stressed out trying to meet the demands of being mothers, wives, singles, employees, committee members, and ministry heads. Some would say being Black and female in America is a major reason for why we have so many stress-related illnesses. We have failed to order our steps in the will of God.

Jesus Himself took out time to rest and recover (Mark 6:30–32). He extended a wonderful invitation to stressed people.

Read Matthew 11:28, and put it in your own words:

Have you refused Christ's gracious invitation? God does require sacrifice, and at times, the work requires long and ongoing effort. Jesus had some advice for the anxious and stressed out.

Put Matthew 6:25–27 in your own words:

Take the time to hear daily the voice of God. Put God first and stop trying to please everybody. Enjoy God's provision and count God's blessings (Philippians 4:4–9). *Sisters, we are too blessed to be stressed!*

GOD'S PLANS TO USE YOU

God's plan for Israel was a grand one. Nehemiah did not share it until he had done his homework. He did not want the skeptics to discourage or hinder it. Some God-sized plans are so large they cannot be believed if we told them. As T. D. Jakes would say, "Get ready! Get ready! Get ready!"

Has God ever given you a plan so grand that you feel it would not be believed if you told it?

What can you see, hear, or perceive that God is telling you to do in these areas:

Personal/family

Church

Community

Nation

World

Have you ever said too much, too soon about a secret plan that God whispered in your ear?

What was the fallout?

WHY CAN'T WE ALL JUST GET ALONG?

Rodney King asked the question, "Why can't we all just get along?" The Scriptures give a simple yet under-acknowledged answer: sin (James 4:1–3). John suggests that all sin is rooted in three desires (1 John 2:15–17):

- The lust of _____ causes us to seek that which satisfies the senses to the neglect of the spirit.

- The lust of _____ causes us to covet or enter into conflict over what is attractive and dazzling to the eye.

- The pride of _____ causes us to value outward symbols of success, fame, position, or status to the neglect of relationships with God, loved ones, and fellow human beings.

These three sins produce seeds that grow in us the weeds that choke out life and unity. God grants permanent and inward peace, love, and joy.

How did Nehemiah respond to the ridicule and mockery of Sanballat, Tobiah, and Geshem?

In Nehemiah 2:19–20, we see he did the following:

1. Exercised wisdom by keeping his cool and responding calmly and intelligently.
2. Stated that they would accomplish their task, for they were servants of the God of heaven.
3. Stated that the work of rebuilding the wall would go forward despite their opposition.
4. Stated that Sanballat, Tobiah, and Geshem had no share, claim, or historic right to be concerned about Jerusalem. In other words, he told them in diplomatic and forthright terms, "Go get yourself some business, because God is on our side, and we will succeed."

ELEMENTS OF A UNIFIED WORK

How were the people able to be so unified as they worked on the wall and gates of Jerusalem? Nehemiah chapter 3 shows us some ingredients. We can use these elements as we seek unity of purpose in our homes and our world.

• **Give the holy first place.** The high priest and other priests began the work at the Towers of Hananel and the Hundred. These areas were located near the temple. They begin with a ceremony consecrating their work to God.

What gate did they repair? (See Nehemiah 3:1.)

The Sheep Gate was where the animals for sacrifice entered. The builders included the daughters of Shallum (Nehemiah 3:12). When work needed to be done, no willing workers were excluded.

- **Value every person's unique contribution.** The builders included men and women of various professions, classes, and backgrounds.

List some of them (Nehemiah 3:1–31):

- **Be willing to do more than your share.** Be diligent and willing to carry more than your load.

Who was singled out for his especially earnest work? (See Nehemiah 3:20.)

Out of all the workers on the walls and gates, Baruch was noted for working *zealously*.

- **Ignore the slackers.** Not everyone is willing to work.

Who were the slackers in this story? (See Nehemiah 3:5.)

The nobles of Tekoa refused to cooperate in the project. Perhaps they thought the work was beneath them. The ordinary citizens of their town completed their assignment and later took other portions of the wall.

- **Follow skilled leadership.** Nehemiah organized the effort masterfully. He knew how to get the job done. When possible, he assigned families to the portion of the wall next to their own houses. This ensured more earnest efforts by the workers, for they would take special care with their own portion of the wall.

How does this effort remind you of the way the body of Christ should function? (See 1 Corinthians 12:14–26.)

CHRIST'S PRAYER FOR ONENESS

Unity was a key element in Jesus Christ's prayer for all believers before His departure from the earth.

Take a moment to read John 17:20–23.

Jesus prayed that God would make us one. He prayed that the church would be a loving community. The world will discover our identity as followers of Christ through our love for God and for one another. As you study today, pray for unity in your world.

During your time of prayer, pray specifically for the following:

___ The unity of the church, which includes many nations and peoples

___ Unity in your community

___ Unity and harmony to permeate your home and the lives of your loved ones

___ Wisdom to help bring unity where you live, work, and serve

___ God' direction to show you what actions you can take to build unity

We sisters let some strange things divide us: hair length and texture, skin color and complexion, attention from men, social status, car models, clothes, and so on. We must resist tendencies to fight with, get mad at, cop an attitude with, mistreat, misuse, or abuse one another. When this happens, sin is bearing its fruit. Sin keeps us jealous and divided. It will take our cooperation with the Holy Ghost to put us back together again. As they used to say, "We came over here in different boats, but we are all in the same boat now."

Sisters, it's all about love. Love is the first brick in the building up of our unity. Overcoming the greatest obstacle to spiritual and physical restoration starts with an understanding that God has been gracious and loving to us, both individually and collectively. If the God of the universe loves us, then we surely ought to love ourselves and each other. Shouldn't we treat God's choice to make us Black, beautiful, women believers in God through Jesus Christ as a marvelous thing?

We are believers in God—let the love of God join us to Him and bind us together for the good of the world and one another. Let us join other people who love our God and prove to all that God is real. They will know we are Christians by our love. Glenda Ngamau exudes this kind of God love.

GLENDA NGAMAU

Glenda Ngamau is a sister who planted her God-given purpose in Chicago in 1989 at Rock of Our Salvation Church through an international missions initiative. *Ngamau*, a Kenyan name, is Glenda's married name—she married her soul mate Wachira Ngamau, and they together planned and have nurtured the success of Pan African Christian Exchange.

While attending Rock of Our Salvation Church, Chicago, Glenda joined a team headed by Wachira, traveling to Kenya to minister and to document the African response to Black Americans. In Kenya, Wachira took Glenda and the other short-term missionaries to various tribes, in order to register a wide range of responses. Everywhere they went, the questions were the same: "Where have you all been?" "Why has it taken you so long to return?" "Why do you have to go back?" "We have enough land here for you all to send for your families!"

They came back to the US and started putting together a team of leaders that would stand behind this mission, PACE. Since then, the Lord has repeatedly affirmed with His blessings and PACE has not lacked a team since 1989. Glenda and Wachira write: "This ministry is responsible for connecting African Americans with brothers and sisters in the African Diaspora, for the express purpose of rebuilding our communities for Christ."

Glenda's passion for widows and orphans remains rooted and committed. The Ngamaus have been raising three children and nurturing their adopted children. She operates the PACE Bible camps for children and youth retreats for teenagers. She also coordinates outreach and programs for short-term missions exposure teams from the US to Kenya.

The Ngamaus have made regular visits to North America but Glenda has sacrificed much time with her immediate and extended family in the US, to carry on the work in Kenya, while Wachira travels primarily, to Canada, where PACE supporters help with orphan care in Africa; to Haiti and beyond, where she has sent her oldest son along with his father to where PACE has rebuilt houses in earthquake-torn and impoverished areas. The African-led mission also goes to the city of Detroit, site of US headquarters and significant supporters, partners, and co-laborers at Rosedale Park Baptist Church. In between, the family has crisscrossed the US, north and south, east and west, to build those relationships that carry missions teams to serve the poor and encourage indigenous ministries of the Diaspora.

Their missions travel to more African countries, the Caribbean, and South America have confirmed to them "that the condition of the Africans of the Diaspora is not much different from Africans themselves."

Since 1995, Glenda and Wachira have been welcoming teens to participate in their exchange and the Lord has been breaking down walls of alienation and isolation that the people of Africa experience wherever they are in the world, and to build up walls of community, unity, and transformation.

Glenda is an example that not only can African Americans be accepted in the lands of their ancestral origin, but both Africans and African Americans have always had a profound impact in each others' countries. She is a lesson in the rich rewards that unity can bring among God's people.

As the Africans and Africans of the Diaspora serve together in each others' countries, they're trying to understand our common past, repair our present condition, and build our future.

LESSON SUMMATION

Nehemiah through God's love achieved his aim of unifying the people to work for restoration. Opposition will come, but as God's servants we can do all things through Christ who strengthens us. Love must be our motive and unity our method to glorify God, our common goal and vision. We must unite for the common good. We must teach our children—girls and boys—to love one another. We must set the standard of harmony in the world.

ꙅDailyꙅDevotions

LESSON FOUR
QUALITIES THAT EXEMPLIFY UNITY

Looking back through the lenses of the New Testament, we can discover several qualities for the church to exemplify Christlike unity. It is a lesson we need to learn, for our unity in love proves to the world that we are the children of God. This week, ask God to help us show these qualities to the world. Read Ephesians 4:1–16; we will focus on verses 2–3.

DAY ONE
CHRISTIAN QUALITY: HUMILITY *(Ephesians 4:2)*
This quality rises out of an understanding that we are unworthy of the love and mercy of God. We must know that we are who we are because of what Christ did for us. Saints are only sinners that have been forgiven.

Where do you stand in relation to this quality? Pray today, asking God to give you true humility.

DAY TWO
CHRISTIAN QUALITY: GENTLENESS OR MEEKNESS *(Ephesians 4:2)*
This quality is the opposite of roughness or thoughtlessness. It is found in people who get angry when others are mistreated but never when they themselves are mistreated.

Where do you stand in relation to this quality? Pray today, asking God to give you gentleness.

DAY THREE
CHRISTIAN QUALITY: PATIENCE OR LONG-SUFFERING
(Ephesians 4:2)

Someone with this quality has a spirit that won't admit defeat, a spirit that won't be broken by trouble or suffering or any disappointment. This quality helps us persist to the end.

Where do you stand in relation to this quality? Pray today, asking God to increase your patience.

DAY FOUR
CHRISTIAN QUALITY: LOVE *(Ephesians 4:2)*

This quality is described in 1 Corinthians 13. The Greeks called it agape love. This love seeks the maximum good for an individual despite his or her behavior.

Where do you stand in relation to this quality? Pray today, asking God to give you agape love.

DAY FIVE
CHRISTIAN QUALITY: PEACE *(Ephesians 4:3)*
This quality relates to letting go of selfish aims to establish and maintain right and appropriate relationships with our fellow earth dwellers.

Where do you stand in relation to this quality? Pray today, asking God to make you a peace-bringer in your world.

NEHEMIAH 4

VITAL VERSES

"They all plotted together to come and fight against Jerusalem and stir up trouble against it. But we prayed to our God and posted a guard day and night to meet this threat." —NEHEMIAH 4:8–9

KEY TERMS

Battle: Conflict between individuals and armies. To achieve restoration, Nehemiah and his people would engage in physical, psychological, and spiritual battle with their enemies. Paul used the idea of battle to describe the Christ follower's life (1 Corinthians 14:8). This kind of battle is spiritual warfare. Nehemiah assured the people that the battle was not theirs but God's and that "God will fight for us" (Nehemiah 4:20).

Weapons: The divine instruments used by Christians for spiritual defense (2 Corinthians 10:1–6). Nehemiah used such instruments as prayer and faith. Our only offensive weapon is the sword of the Spirit, which is the Word of God (Romans 8:37–39; Ephesians 6:11–17).

$\mathcal{S}$ometimes you have to fight evil. Sometimes the heat of the Christian battle is so intense that I have to tell the devil where to go. What about you? Truth is, the devil is so subtle and deceptive that he makes wrong seem right. Truth is, our people have to stop believing and acting on the lies that have been told to us. When we believe lies we become vulnerable to the father of lies.

Sometimes we have to fight. But don't be deceived; we are not fighting a physical battle. The battle for the hearts of our people is spiritual. The force against us is great, for it destroys the purity and innocence of our children, it kills or imprisons our men, it prevents us from being brilliant lights for our Lord. Listening to the statistics, I know that the devil fears our potential strength as people fully aligned with the will God.

Remember, nothing of the devil's is worth having. We know that greater is the power of God within us than the forces outside God's will. Sometimes we have to fight evil, and when we do, we fight back to back— we fight to win. The weapons we use must be spiritual, and must include every part of us. We must pray, watch, fight, and then *keep on praying*. Not for ourselves alone, but for the world to which God has sent us to be light and salt.

This week we will look at how Nehemiah and the Jewish people overcame the internal and external enemies to their restoration. We will discover how to win victories against the plans, plots, and intentions of our enemies. We will discover the necessity to work, fight, and pray. We will be encouraged to guard our section of life's wall. We will learn some steps to overcome discouragement. We will put on the full armor of God.

Take time now to read today's main Scripture, Nehemiah 4.

We find Nehemiah surrounded by his enemies. They began with ridicule and slander and moved to a secret plot to attack Israel and kill the people. Every attack of their enemies was turned away by

God-empowered wisdom, discernment, and spiritual weaponry wrapped up in prayer. The threats increased, and it became essential to carry the weapons of battle at all times. Israel's experiences help us learn the weapons and actions necessary for us to be victorious in our battles against evil.

ATTACKED WITH LIES AND PUT-DOWNS: NEHEMIAH 4:1–3

Sanballat and Tobiah, Israel's enemies, were up to no good again. Sanballat, in front of the Samaritan army and its allies, scorned and ridiculed his Israelite neighbors. Anger ruled their hearts—their tongues poured out bitter poison (James 3:7–8). Walking about like prideful peacocks, their mockery and slander were cover-ups for their own insecurities, jealousy, and envy. Their words contradicted what their eyes could easily see. Stuck with an old image of Israel, they could not recognize the new creation God was making in Jerusalem. Still, words can wound spirits, which are much more fragile than bones.

The forces of evil manifested themselves in the question of Sanballat: "What are those feeble Jews doing? Will they restore their wall and gates? Will they offer sacrifices? Will they finish in a day? Can they bring the stones back to life from those heaps of rubble—burned as they are?" He wanted to put down the people of Israel, their abilities, their goals, their resources. How could they succeed when they had little or nothing with which to work?

Tobiah jumped in and made fun of the work the people were doing. He said, "What they are building—if even a fox climbed up on it, he would break down their wall of stones!"

THE WEAPON OF PRAYER: NEHEMIAH 4:4–6

The builders were putting forth their best efforts, yet the hateful words of their enemies must have bothered them. Nehemiah's response was to use the ready weapon of a believer—he prayed. His prayer put in words the pain of his people: "Hear us, O our God, for we are despised." They were detested, despised, and hated because of their commitment to be faithful to their God and His unique and holy laws.

Some of us don't know what to make of this prayer of Nehemiah. Sounds like he was pretty ticked off. He maintained his cool when personally confronted (Nehemiah 2:19–20), but when confronted with ridicule for his people he lost it. How would you feel if such things were said of your children or loved ones? What if the N word had been used? Sounds like Nehemiah wanted God to pull out the BIG guns.

Prayers of the Old Testament include some that call on God for revenge against one's enemies, such as Psalm 64:7–8. Jewish law was designed to stop people from taking excessive revenge for a personal offense. For example, the law "an eye for and eye, and a tooth for tooth" was to prevent a person from putting out both the eyes of (or even killing) the person who had put out one of his eyes. Did Nehemiah's prayer go beyond this standard in the Law of Moses?

Harriet Tubman, the "Black Moses," once told the story of how she prayed constantly for her slave master's conversion and change of heart. After countless prayers, she discovered that her master had plans to put her "in the chain gang to de far South." She then prayed that God would take her master's life. Shortly thereafter, her master died. For the rest of her life, she was burdened with guilt that she had prayed such a prayer.

Both Harriet and Nehemiah spoke to God out of their heartbreak and pain. We discover that we can be honest to God about our hurts, anger, doubts, and lack of willingness to obey and follow. Any relationship is strengthened when we can express our emotions and still be embraced by forgiving love. All prayers should end in, "nevertheless thy will be done." God's will always lines up with God's love, truth, and mercy.

How should we respond to our enemies? (See Matthew 5:38–48.)

It's hard to do, but we are to pray for God to change their hearts and for our ability to forgive injustices against us. God loves us, and when we fail to turn our hearts toward the good, we will be appropriately repaid by Him; the same is true for our enemies. (See Romans 12:17–21.)

The way that we keep things in proper perspective is to remember the countless times we have been forgiven by God. The way that Christ helped us see this clearly was to tell us that as we forgive, so will we be forgiven.

THE WEAPON OF IDENTITY

History records hateful acts against the Jews, from Bible times up to the stories of Hitler's death camps. Hatred of Jews continues today. Nehemiah had achieved all the markings of personal success, but as with similar forms of hatred, he was often reminded in subtle and sometimes stinging ways that he was a Jew. Millionaire superstar Bill Cosby once told Bryant Gumbel in a *Today Show* interview that, with all his success and wealth, he could walk out of the NBC studio and be refused a cab because of the color of his skin. We know where you're coming from, Dr. Cosby.

Nehemiah refused to believe the lies. He took comfort and pride in his identity as a Jew. They were God's chosen people! They were at work restoring the holy city of Jerusalem! He urged the people, "Don't be afraid of them. *Remember the Lord*" (Nehemiah 4:14). Their task was so worthy and important that it towered over their lives, and the taunts of neighbors paled into insignificance.

Maya Angelou, who walks and talks like an African queen, made a statement in an *Essence* magazine interview that makes a sister grin with pride:

If you happen to have the blessing to have been born Black and the extra blessing to have been born a female and an American, then each filament of power you have, you have laid it and layered it carefully, not like someone from a family whose name makes people shiver in the marketplace—Rockefeller, DuPont, Kennedy. . . . So I would say the power I have comes directly from being a descendant of people whose powerful history makes me humble. I would think, if I had been born anything other than . . . a Black American woman, that I had done something wrong. . . .

What is your reaction to Maya's statement?

Has the world mistreated and/or undervalued you because you are a Christian and/or African American and/or a woman? Give an example.

God called African American women to be believers before the world was made (Ephesians 1:4).

What is God's view of us—God's creation? (See Genesis 1:31.)

We are blessed to be born Black American women. Our experiences have given us a unique way to look at and live out our faith in God.

A PLOT TO DESTROY: NEHEMIAH 4:6-9, 11

The slander and false accusations of their enemies only strengthened the Jews' resolve to work. In a short time, the wall was up to half its intended height, and they were continuing to close the gaps. On hearing this, the two amigos, their enemies, came up with a plot. They joined together Samaritans from the north and the Ammonites from the east, the Arabians from the south and the Ashdodites from the west. Wow! The enemies surrounded the Israelites. They plotted to catch the workers off guard, surprise them, and kill them.

The secret plot was uncovered, and the workers with Nehemiah responded by calling upon the Lord Almighty, commander of the universe. Nehemiah set up a system that allowed for a 24-hour watch around the city. His strategy was to pray, watch, and keep on praying—not in that order, but simultaneously (at the same time) and continuously (all the time).

This lesson has covered several ways evil attacks us: lies and putdowns, ridicule, and plots for destruction.

What are some other attributes of evil and the evil one mentioned in the Scriptures below?

Job 1:7-12

John 8:44

Job 2:7

Zechariah 3:1

Matthew 4:3

Matthew 13:19, 38–39

John 10:10

1 Peter 5:8

The attributes you discovered about evil and the evil one are that he is the adversary, tempter, devourer, accuser, liar, destroyer, murderer, slanderer, and thief. Israel's enemies are filling out the job requirements pretty well so far.

Considering the above attributes of evil, have you encountered true evil?

We trust that God, who is wise, will direct and protect us.

THE WEAPON OF ALERTNESS

I have served as a chaplain for the members of the 117th Air Refueling Wing of the Alabama Air National Guard. Our mission: to refuel military aircraft in midair. Because this job is critical for the military's mission to protect and serve our nation, we are told to maintain "alert" at all times. We must be prepared to serve, bags packed and family matters in order. The duty of every member is, through training and vigilance, to maintain worldwide mobility—ready to go wherever we are sent to serve.

The Christian soldier must keep alert also to plots that seek to destroy the mission of the church of Jesus Christ. The places we are directed to serve and protect include our home, church, community, anywhere we have influence. Christians are to maintain worldwide mobility—to go where God sends us and do and say as the Spirit of Christ commands. Our mission is to reclaim and proclaim the Way through Christ to life abundant and eternal. Are you prayerful and alert—on watch and waiting to do as God commands?

ATTACKED BY DISCOURAGEMENT: NEHEMIAH 4:10-15

The Jews who lived outside the city walls, closer to the encroaching nations, were constantly reporting talk about the ferocity and evil intentions of their enemies. The fear of attack and sheer physical fatigue from the difficulty and pace of the work caused the workers to become overwhelmed and discouraged.

Nehemiah continued battle preparation, putting people at the lowest points and exposed areas in the wall to give the appearance of being prepared for battle. He urged families to accept the responsibility to protect their own. They were equipped with military weaponry—swords, bows, and spears. Nehemiah stood before the people to deliver a speech to his frightened, weary, and discouraged workers. The message gives us some fine advice along with preparing us for handling discouragement, fear, fatigue, and spiritual attack. The four points in his message are outlined below.

Read Nehemiah 4:14, and fill in the blanks:

1. Don't be _____ .

2. _____ the Lord!

3. The Lord is _____ and _____ !

4. Fight for your _____ , your _____ , and your _____ , your _____ , and your _____ !

Good message, Nehemiah.

Based on his message to the workers, in what ways will you overcome future bouts with discouragement, fear, and weariness?

THE WEAPON OF ENCOURAGEMENT

Nehemiah had a ministry of encouragement, and we, too, are to be encouragers—cheerleaders for one another.

What are ways you will carry out your ministry of encouragement?

When Israel's enemies got the news, heard of the fortitude and courage of the "feeble" Jews, and saw the city preparing fearlessly, they rethought the situation. Israel's God once again put a major kink in their plans, so they backed down and backed off.

Nehemiah's encouragement helped the builders overcome their fear. Fear had driven them to stop their work. Fear about threats often stops or blocks our progress toward our goals. Overcoming fear and discouragement, the Israelite builders got back to the task at hand. God again came through for His people. Say amen, somebody!

THE WEAPON OF VIGILANCE: NEHEMIAH 4:16–23

Nehemiah, a former cupbearer turned motivational speaker, architect, wall-builder, and then military commander, devised a plan to ensure that he and the builders were always prepared and the people always protected. He set up an impromptu military camp and fortress. Note the responsibilities assigned each person. Every person had a job, either building or protecting. Nehemiah had at his side a trumpeter who could call the people for battle at a moment's notice. Nehemiah reminded them that the battle was not theirs but the Lord's. God would fight for them. Nehemiah and his relatives (brothers), his personal workers, and bodyguards never took off their weapons. Nehemiah's army was fully prepared for their enemies.

Eternal vigilance is the price we pay for our Christian liberty. We must pray, watch, fight, and pray more. We must use the tools that Nehemiah recommended to his nation to overcome discouragement and battle fatigue. Additionally, we must put on the full armor of God because those who follow Jesus are targets of the enemy. The force of evil seeks our surrender. Our Teacher, Savior, and Lord, Jesus Christ, has laid out the way to victory before us.

In what ways are you being vigilant to protect your family? Are you helping them to prepare for life's spiritual battles?

THE FULL ARMOR OF GOD

God has left us with the weapons to win the battles on this side of eternity. We wrestle against forces impossible to defeat without the armament supplied by God. We have heard of these weapons time and time again. Without them, we are sitting ducks for the tricks of those who carry out evil. With them, we experience victory. The weapons of our warfare are found in Ephesians 6:10–20.

Our weapons are

- the belt of _____ ,
- the breastplate of _____ ,
- the readiness of the gospel of _____ ,
- the shield of _____ ,
- the helmet of _____ , and
- the sword of the _____ .

Be _____ , and always keep _____ .

Sisters, there's a war going on—to win the hearts, minds, strength, and spirits of the people of God. Determined forces seek to rob us of finding and living a good life on this earth. Stand guard, protect the ones you love—God is on our side. Pray, watch, fight, and pray some more. The sweet but deceptive music of the world seeks to lull us to sleep and away from our duties.

The greatest tragedy would be to ignore the power of God to deliver us. To deny that power is to deny the power of God to create the world or raise Jesus Christ from the dead. God spoke the word, and the world came to be out of nothing. The greatest evidence of the force of heaven ever manifested on earth was the resurrection of Christ Jesus from the dead. *God can do anything — anything but fail.*

Sister—soldier of the Cross—stand! Don't you get weary of the battles of life. Our God has laid before us His own armor. With the weapons we have, we do our part on the walls and gates that protect and defend our daughters, sons, mothers, fathers, spouses, homes, and, yes, ourselves. We invest all we can for the cause and truths of our Savior. If we stand, if we watch, fight, and pray, God will fight with and for us. We are witnesses of the countless times that Christ has rescued us from the heat of battle and poured into our lives the cool, refreshing, and perpetual waters of God's love, grace, and mercy. Our commander in chief is the defender of truth and righteousness.

Excerpt from *Power Suit* by Sharon Norris Elliott:

> Have you heard of the armor of God—and attempted to implement it? We can find ourselves down more than up . . . shaking our heads, wondering what hit us. The armor doesn't seem to be working as it should.
>
> Our defeats in spiritual battles are not because of any defect in the Power Suit, but because of problems with the fit. . . . A Christian who knows how to use the Word of God effectively is the most lethal weapon to Satan on the face of the earth. Satan and his demons quake in fear before Jesus who is the living Word of God. (See John 1:1, 14, and James 2:19.) When we are in our full Power Suit, Satan can't tell us from Christ. . . . When dealing with the enemy, we should sound like Jesus did when Satan tempted Him and out of our mouths should come, "It is written."
>
> We are that lethal weapon when we "pull" sin from our lives by accepting Christ's forgiving work He finished at Calvary, "push" the Word of God into ourselves daily, "tap" into the mind of Christ by allowing the Holy Spirit to direct us as to exactly how to use the Word, and then "aim and fire" accurately, applying the Word with wisdom, reverence, love, and respect. With all the other pieces of the armor, we have discussed how they may not fit because of the

other junk we haven't yet taken off. In the case of our weaponry, that which gets in the way of the Word of God is our inability to use it properly.

Second Timothy 2:15 says, *"Do your best to present yourself to God as one approved, a workman who does not need to be ashamed and who **correctly handles the word of truth**"* (emphasis added).

The words *do your best* in the above verse are translated "study" in the King James Version and are derived from the Greek word *spoudazo*, which means to use speed, to make effort, be prompt or earnest, give diligence, and labor. To show yourself as one approved means that you are acceptable because you have been tried or tested. You are a workman who has toiled in order to pass the truth along to others accurately.

If we want to be good at anything, we must spend time with it. From the age of 5 until I was 16, I took classical piano lessons. Every Thursday, I sat at a piano in Mrs. Dolly Perry's backyard room as she and my John Thompson books taught me to play. Halfway through the levels of those red books, Mrs. Perry added studies from *Hanon the Virtuoso Pianist*. My fingers ran up and down the keyboard playing scales and performing exercises.

At home, I'd practice a half-hour every day. By the time I entered high school and stopped taking lessons, I could read any piece of music; perform the works of the masters like Bach, Beethoven, and Chopin; and accompany my church's children's choir. I eventually progressed to composing my own praise choruses and leading the praise and worship time at church. Building bit by bit over those 11 years made me skillful on the piano. Studying God's Word makes us skillful in its use; to reach a decent level of proficiency takes the same kind of diligence as my years at the piano.

"All right," you say. "I understand that the Bible is God's Word and God's Word is my sword, the number one weapon I can use against Satan, my enemy, in the spiritual warfare I'm in. I'm convinced that I need to study my Bible so I can properly use it as a weapon. . . ."

I submit to you that we are dressed in our godly work clothes in order to do the work of the kingdom. We do the work of the kingdom by staying in communication with our Leader and following His directives.

The final verse of our key passage about the Power Suit is Ephesians 6:18 (KJV). This gives us our marching orders. It says, *"Praying always with all prayer and supplication in the Spirit, and watching thereunto with all perseverance and supplication for all saints."* Basically, as long as we stay tuned in to God, we'll take our stand victoriously. . . . Communication is key to the control of the battlefield of life. If we are not receiving clear and prompt descriptions of events transpiring, nor receiving our orders in a timely manner, the mission of our lives will end in disastrous defeat. Communication is key to the control of the battlefield of life.

Prayer is communication with heaven. Ephesians 6:18 tells us we are to be involved in prayer, supplication, watching (being alert), and persevering. ***Prayer:*** Prayer is simply communication with God that works throughout your life. It's a two-way conversation in which we must be careful to listen to what God wants us to know. He impresses His thoughts to you. You listen and you respond to Him. . . .

Make prayer a consistent aspect of your Christian life. Listen to what God says to you through His

Word and in your mind and Spirit. If you've been out of communication, God's waiting with open arms for you to return.

Ladies, wear the Power Suit with purpose. Take off all the junk that causes the pieces not to fit. Wrap snugly into the good foundation garment of the belt of truth. Suit up in the breastplate of righteousness. Slip on the matching shoes of the preparation of the gospel of peace. Hold up the convertible, carryall shield of faith. Crown yourself with the helmet of salvation. Accessorize with the sword of the Spirit. And don't forget to pray. Dress up and move out!

LESSON SUMMATION

Every weapon used by Israel's enemies was overcome by the Israelites' faith in the might of God. Their enemies used lies, put-downs, and intimidation, but God's people achieved the victory by recognizing their unique identity before God. They trusted God's estimation of their potential and not their enemy's estimation. They were despised by many nations throughout their history, but they were deeply loved and provided for by their God. Like Nehemiah, we must pray when we are ridiculed, but the content of our prayers must be dictated by the teaching of our Savior, Jesus Christ.

Life offers us countless reasons to be discouraged and to give up, but we can have the encouragement of knowing that God will fight for us. His love for us is steadfast. He equips us with spiritual weapons and divine protection. Will you put on the whole armor of God? We have past testimony, present assurance, and future faith that no weapon formed against us will succeed. Christ has achieved the victory; we must pray, fight, watch, and keep on praying. We stay on constant alert, ready to recruit others to serve with us in the army of God, the side that always wins. After all, the battle is not ours; it is the Lord's.

‿❧DAILY❧DEVOTIONS

LESSON FIVE
THE SOURCE OF OUR ARMOR

This week, we will give thanks for the protection, power, and gift of God's armor we wear to win the battles of the Christian life. We will focus on Ephesians 6:10–13 for our main Scripture.

DAY ONE
THE NATURE OF OUR WARFARE
Read Ephesians 6:10–13.

Today, be empowered by God in communion with Christ Jesus. Do not be fooled; the enemies we are struggling with are not physical—they can be material, but they exist in the invisible spiritual realm. We cannot win using our own might. The might of the all-powerful God is your tool against the enemies of truth, righteousness, and love. For your protection, the full armor of God—God's own armor—has been given to you. (See Isaiah 59:15–18.) We go to overcome the realm of darkness, the "powers and principalities," with God's light. Stand fearlessly against the forces of evil in life's battlefield.

Write a prayer thanking God for His power at work in your life. Thank Him for at least three things that are evidence of His power.

DAY TWO
THE BELT OF TRUTH AND BREASTPLATE OF RIGHTEOUSNESS
Read Ephesians 6:14.

Paul compares our spiritual weapons to the weapons of a soldier. Christian soldiers are to be girded with truth (Isaiah 11:5). Christian truth includes the good news of God's salvation through Christ Jesus and living lives of truth, honesty, and integrity. The breastplate of righteousness (Isaiah 59:17) is the assurance that, no matter what others say about us, we have been made righteous—justified by Christ (Ephesians 4:24). Our character should reflect our imitation of the character, the personality of Christ (Ephesians 5:1–2).

How have you experienced God's truth and righteousness in the last 24 hours?

DAY THREE
THE SHOES OF THE GOSPEL OF PEACE AND THE SHIELD OF FAITH
Read Ephesians 6:15–16.

In the midst of the chaos, confusion, and division, we walk through life ready, willing, and able to freely offer through word and lifestyle the good news of the pathway to peace within and with God (Isaiah 52:7). The body-length shield of faith and trust in God protects us from the flaming arrows of Satan. Faith enables us to see beyond the natural and see our present victories and final victory in Jesus Christ (Hebrews 11:1).

How have you experienced and shared God's peace in the last 24 hours?

How has your faith protected you from Satan's arrows in that same period?

DAY FOUR
THE HELMET OF SALVATION AND THE SWORD OF THE SPIRIT
Read Ephesians 6:17.

While the Christian soldier puts on every previous piece of armor, she is unable with all her heavy armor to put on the helmet of salvation and the sword of the Spirit. She receives these items from her armor bearer. Once we confess, accept, believe, and follow Him, we push back doubts about and doubters of our possession of God's precious gift of eternal life (1 Thessalonians 5:8–9; Jude 24). The Word of God is our only offensive weapon—we use it when we must lead the charge against evil. When evil threatens us, we must trust in the message of the gospel and proclaim its power in us and through us (Matthew 10:19–20; John 1:14).

How have you used the sword of the Spirit (the Word of God) to fight evil in the last 24 hours?

DAY FIVE
ALL PRAYER AND SUPPLICATION ALL THE TIME
Read Ephesians 6:18–20.

The battle is fought and won by maintaining communication (communion) with the command center—heaven. The heated battles require that our hearts be positioned and open to speak to and to hear from heaven and earth's commander. When we are under assault, and we always are, we need the reinforcement of prayer partners—the body of Christ. We must remain alert, praying for our fellow soldiers of the cross. We must pray for our spiritual leaders, who are more often at the front lines and thus are easy targets of the evil one.

List two people on the front lines for whom you will pray today.

LESSON SIX

Cry Out for Justice

NEHEMIAH 5

VITAL VERSES

"Now the men and their wives raised a great outcry against their Jewish brothers. . . . 'Although we are of the same flesh and blood as our countrymen and though our sons are as good as theirs, yet we have to subject our sons and daughters to slavery. Some of our daughters have already been enslaved, but we are powerless, because our fields and our vineyards belong to others.'"
— NEHEMIAH 5:1, 5

KEY TERMS

Justice: The gauge for benefits and penalties of living in society. Justice is a chief characteristic of God. It is the correcting of conditions and societal imbalances that cause injustice and inequality (Psalm 10:17–18). When we do justice, we are representatives of God's will (Isaiah 59:15–16). Justice and righteousness go together. In the New Testament, Christians are called to seek righteousness. We live righteous lives when we carry out justice.

Fear of God: Refers to the reverence that rules those who live for God, and the lack of it that characterizes the lives of those who fail to be obedient (Psalm 34:11; 2 Corinthians 5:11). It includes a healthy respect for God's ability to correct and punish those who stray from Him. The phrase "fear of God" is often used by Nehemiah to explain his choices (Nehemiah 5:9; 5:15; 7:2).

On December 1, 1955, Rosa Parks, in defiance of the Jim Crow laws, refused to give up her seat to a White passenger on a bus in Montgomery, Alabama. You will recall that Rosa had a mentor in Septima Poinsette Clark, who stood fast on her mission. Like Clark before her, Parks suffered for her action on the behalf of human justice. She was arrested for her refusal to give up her seat.

The arrest of this humble, yet determined African American woman of faith sparked a bus boycott and a movement for justice and equality that changed the future of Black Americans and life in America forever—and has had an impact beyond these shores. What made her do it? Rosa Parks believed that God is just and stands on the side of the poor, oppressed, and downtrodden. She believed that the just laws of God overrule the unjust laws of humanity.

By the grace of God, the civil rights movement and the changes it brought permitted many of us to escape the disadvantages of poverty. Still, studies show that criminal justice continues to give a raw deal to the poor and members of minority (rising majority) groups. School systems in poor communities are stuck with outdated books, lower salaries for workers, and run-down facilities. Unfair lending practices still keep qualified African Americans from being approved for home loans—or target them for poor practices that attack their finances. The number of individuals who are unable to afford medical coverage has continued to rise. Even with hard-fought changes in laws and systems, a large percentage of those most affected by injustice and the poverty caused by injustice are Black women and children.

Often you and I are confronted with subtle and not-so-subtle forms of discrimination. Because we know the problem so well, Black American Christians are uniquely able to call America to God's standard of justice for the poor, the stranger, and the disadvantaged. Taking care of the poor is not something God asks us to do as a kindness for "extra credit." It is commanded; it is a part of basic *justice*. We must join the chorus of all who advocate justice. Do not just feed the poor; fight boldly for justice in America. Why should we do it? God is just and demands justice. We are called to be imitators of God.

TRUE-LIFE DRAMA

In Nehemiah chapter 5, Nehemiah came face to face with injustice in his homeland. We will discover how and why he demanded that those in power and those with money treat their fellow citizens justly. We will learn how he and others in his family and administration showed compassion for the poor in their nation. We will consider how and why we have a responsibility to act justly.

This portion of the story of Judah's restoration is worthy of being a criminal-justice television show or movie. We need someone like Denzel Washington in the lead role as the attorney for the downtrodden. Before the camera rolls, let's get the background to this heart-tugging true-life drama.

Take time now to read the main Scripture for this lesson, Nehemiah 5.

THE PLIGHT OF THE POOR: NEHEMIAH 5:1–5

The work of clearing the charred rubble and rebuilding Jerusalem's wall and gates took the men of Judah away from their families and everyday provision for them. The women were left with the responsibility of caring for the family and the land. The country was experiencing famine. The Jewish people also had to pay taxes (tribute) to the Persian government. A crisis was inevitable.

The people raised an outcry. Both the men and the women came to Nehemiah and wanted their concerns addressed. What was a mere economic downturn on one side of town had caused a desperate depression on the poor side of town. With the compassion of loan sharks, the rich of their nation saw the situation as an opportunity to strengthen their stock portfolios, to further line their silk pockets.

They were loaning money to starving Jews and when they couldn't repay it, the poor were forced to sell their children into slavery. The men and their wives couldn't hold their peace, so they filed their complaints in Nehemiah's "court" of justice. Three different groups of farmers made complaint:

1. One group did not have enough food to feed their large families. These were probably people who had no land for collateral to get a loan for food and taxes. Some scholars translate the passage from the Hebrew to say, "We have to pledge our sons and daughters in order to get grain, so we can eat and stay alive."

2. Another group had taken out loans on their homes, lands, and crops and still did not have enough food. They stated that the famine had made a bad situation worse.

3. Another group had to borrow against their property to pay taxes to Persia. Because they were not able to pay back their loans, they were being forced to sell their children into slavery. Already some of their daughters had been sold to be concubines or sexual slaves.

The third group pointed out how the wealthy failed to see their children and poor children as equal. They had no regard for the fact that they were of the same nation, blood, and racial heritage. In other words, "Give a brother (or a sister) a break." The poor were saying in so many words, "Governor Nehemiah, it just ain't right," or "Where is justice?" Something within them rejected the idea that they were of less value because they had less money. They ended their argument with a telling statement: *"We are powerless, because our fields and our vineyards belong to others"* (Nehemiah 5:5; *author's emphasis*). Their bootstraps "to pull themselves up by," even their *boots*, did not exist.

IN CONFLICT WITH GOD'S LAWS

What happened violated laws of God regarding the poor and disadvantaged. Mosaic Law required generosity to the poor and needy in the Israelite community (Deuteronomy 15:7–11). God had delivered Israel in their hours of greatest need—the bondage in Egypt and the recent Babylonian exile—and they should treat others likewise. They were always to remember that they were once slaves and should therefore treat their servants with dignity (Deuteronomy 15:15). Their God, unlike the gods of other nations, comes to the defense of the poor and needy (Psalm 82:1–4). The laws commanded that every seven years, all debts were to be forgiven (Deuteronomy 15:1–6). These same laws forbade Israelites charging interest to poor members of their community (Exodus 22:25–27).

A PROPER RESPONSE TO INJUSTICE: NEHEMIAH 6:6–8

After hearing the complaints of the poor, Nehemiah wanted to "go off" on the nobles and officials. Nehemiah had a temper, for his memoirs note a time when he lost his patience with those who persisted in disobeying the Law (Nehemiah 13:23–27). But this time, he took time to cool off and responded calmly and intelligently ("my mind thought with itself") before bringing up charges against the wealthy lenders. Nehemiah was also hurt that the Israelites would take advantage of one another. One translation of his words puts it this way: "My heart was broken within me." Nehemiah, being one of the wealthy members (if not the wealthiest) of the community, decided to confront folk with whom he may one day "play a round of golf." His sense of justice overruled any class loyalty (Exodus 23:6). He was all about doing the right thing.

Privately, Nehemiah brought charges against the nobles and officials to no avail. So Nehemiah took his case against the lenders before the people in a public meeting. His powerful arguments in his presentation to the citizens began with how he and his brothers had responded to the plight of the poor. They had used their own money, as they were able, to *buy back their people from slavery* to the Gentiles. The accused had sold their people *into slavery* and Nehemiah's family had to buy them back. In other words, "We can expect our enemies, who don't know our God, to enslave people for debt and keep them in bondage; but it is our obligation to keep our people out of slavery to foreigners." These statements by Nehemiah left the accused speechless — "they could find nothing to say" (Nehemiah 5:8).

DEMAND FOR JUSTICE: NEHEMIAH 5:9–12

Nehemiah continued his argument by stating something like, "Wrong is wrong, and you folks are just plain wrong. Even if you have no conscience, you should at least fear God's judgment. Your deeds are a poor testimony to the world and a poor testimony of what the people of God are all about. These requirements of collateral must stop now. Give them back their means of livelihood and all the interest you have collected." The truth and merits of Nehemiah's case are plain enough even for Stevie Wonder to see!

Look at Nehemiah 5:12. In your own words, what is the response of the accused persons?

Yes, under the powerful pressure of God's word through Nehemiah and the witnesses assembled, they agreed to pay back and return the property and interest they had amassed.

Social activists say that "oppressors" never freely give up their power. That was certainly true in our history.

Do you agree or disagree? Give an example.

REAPING WHAT WE SOW: NEHEMIAH 5:12B-13

The wealthy of the community reluctantly agreed to do what Nehemiah and the laws of God demanded. Nehemiah required them to make an oath to God before the priests. He sealed the agreement with a symbolic gesture that the ancients believed made sure God would carry out the action. Small personal items would be carried in the folds of one's garment as we carry things in our pockets today. A person would loose the garment by taking off his belt and shouting, "Empty." Nehemiah shook out everything in the folds of his garment. The curse would happen if the nobles and officials failed to keep their pledge. Like those they wronged, they would lose their home, land, and possessions. All of those assembled, probably the poor and not so poor, shouted, "Amen." The nobles and officials kept their vows. You can't blame them, can you?

A WEALTHY AND HONEST POLITICIAN? NEHEMIAH 5:14-19

Nehemiah for the first time mentioned that he had been appointed governor of Judah by King Artaxerxes. His first term lasted 12 years (445–433 B.C.). Later, he would return to serve another term. When Nehemiah wrote this part of his memoir, he added how he did everything within his power to serve his people with equality, justice, and generosity.

His kindness stood in stark contrast to the treatment of the people by the governors who preceded him.

Check the boxes that characterize the behavior of those governors (Nehemiah 5:15).

❑ They demanded heavy local taxation to support their administration.

❑ The assistants treated the people poorly and lorded over them.

❑ They got an allotment of food for their family and administration.

How did Nehemiah's family and administration treat the people?
(See Nehemiah 5:16–18.)

Check the statements that apply.

❑ They worked alongside the people to rebuild the city walls and gates.

❑ They did not acquire land.

❑ They never demanded the food allotment of the governor's family and administration.

❑ They did not place a heavy tax burden on the people.

Why was Nehemiah's administration different from the administrations of governors that preceded him? (See Nehemiah 5:15.)

Yes, Nehemiah, himself, did all that he demanded of his people—out of fear and reverence for God. He was a man of wealth. He was able, from his own pocket, to feed over 150 Jewish and Persian officials and visiting dignitaries daily at his table in the governor's residence. He refused to take his "salary" as governor because the people could not afford the additional financial burden. They needed everything they could get to feed their families, survive periodic famines, and pay the taxes of the empire.

Nehemiah is an example of a politician who served both his God and his people faithfully and honestly.

What were the causes of crisis in Jerusalem? Check the correct box below:

❑ Persian taxes

❑ Laziness of the poor

❑ Famine or drought conditions in the land
❑ The rich taking advantage of the poor

All of the above are correct, except the one about laziness.

The circumstances that cause poverty include major things like lack of hope, lack of a living wage, health crises, poor job skills, dysfunctional families, and broken homes. Many people are only a few paychecks away from homelessness. These things certainly have caused high rates of poverty among African Americans; women and children are particularly affected by poverty in America.

What ground to stand on did the poor have when they made their complaints? (See Deuteronomy 15:7–11 and Psalm 82:1–4.)

God is just; He expects His people to act justly. The poor have the same needs and rights as those who have more material goods. In this story, the poor were of the same blood and race as their wealthier sisters and brothers. The Sinai covenant was central to their faith. These laws demanded that they remember how they were once mistreated as slaves and how God mercifully delivered them from Egyptian bondage.

What can Nehemiah's responses teach us about how we should respond to complaints of injustice? (See Nehemiah 5:9–14.)

What are three things the Lord requires of us? (See Micah 6:8.)

The New Testament uses the word *righteous* to explain how Christians should live (see the key term *justice*). We are righteous when we treat our neighbor justly. We are just when we treat others as we would want others to treat us if we were in their shoes.

What is the "Golden Rule"? (See Luke 6:31.)

Write it below in your own words.

The rich in this situation in Jerusalem had no compassion for the poor. Is money the root of all evil? (See 1 Timothy 6:10.)

No, the *love* of money is the root of all kinds of evil. Nehemiah was a man of great wealth, and he and his relatives used their money to help the poor. Nehemiah modeled and demanded honesty in his administration. One scholar, Walter Brueggemann, notes that in Psalm 82 the gods of other nations are put on trial. However, our God, the God of Israel, defends the weak.

Read Psalm 82 and list some of the qualities of those whom God defends.

Jesus gave His mission statement to His home "church" (Luke 4:18–20). The Spirit of God was upon Him; He was anointed to do some specific things:

- To preach the good news to _____.
- To proclaim _____ to the _____.
  and recovery of sight for the _____.
- To release the _____.
- To _____ the year of God's favor

Considering the nature of God, what should be the nature of God's people in regard to justice and righteousness?

God's mighty deliverance of Israel from bondage and many similar actions on their behalf proved that God was on the side of the poor and oppressed. Therefore, their laws were designed to make sure that they defended and gave relief for the poor and defenseless in their community of faith.

What are three principles African Americans can learn from the Israelite understanding of the laws of God, the nature of God, and our response to injustices?

Israel remembered her history of bondage and used that memory to determine her present and shape her future.

Name two kinds of "bonds" that you've experienced.

How is God able to deliver you?

Africans enslaved in America believed in the justice of God. The songs they sang expressed what they believed about the nature of God. I think of "Go Down Moses," "Heaven, Heaven," and the songs used by slaves to leave messages as they escaped bondage, like "Steal Away" and "Swing Low, Sweet Chariot."

Can you think of one or more of these songs?

Like the slaves, my experiences and the Scriptures have taught me— rather, convinced me—of the justice and love of God.

Why do you think African Americans—African American women, particularly —are today lovers of justice?

Where do you see injustice today?

What are some practical ways you and your family can assist God in promoting justice?

WE ARE NOT SATISFIED

The cry of our people since coming to the shores of America can best be articulated with the words of Dr. Martin Luther King Jr.:

> "We are not satisfied, and we will be not satisfied until 'justice rolls down like waters and righteousness like a mighty stream'" (quoting Amos 5:24).

Dr. King called America to live up to our own founding documents that stated that we were "one nation under God."

This one nation was, as Abraham Lincoln explained in his Gettysburg Address, "conceived in liberty, and dedicated to the proposition that all men are created equal." When these words were written, our ancestors were still in bondage, and Blacks and women did not have the right to vote.

Some Americans cry out for our country to go back to the time of the founding fathers—a time when we lived more faithfully under God. African Americans view any suggestions to go back to a pre–civil rights era not as an idealistic dream but as a certifiable nightmare. We do not want to go back to a time when we, because of skin color or gender, were not able to exercise our right to vote. We are wary of those who continue to seek to overturn the right to vote or to hinder the results that have come with the right to vote.

We do not want to go back to a time when Blacks did not serve as city police chiefs, state legislators, CEOs of Fortune 500 companies, US Congress members, White House Cabinet members, and President!

We want to go forward into a future where all people are able to get a fair shake in the criminal justice system, all children get a quality education, and racial profiling does not exist. We want to go forward into a future where glass ceilings do not hold back employees because of racism or gender prejudices. We have come a long way, ladies, but you and I know that we must continue to go forward because our God is just and expects us to advocate justice in our world.

As we press forward, we need to remember the sacrifices of those in our past who have advocated before us.

NANNIE HELEN BURROUGHS

Excerpted from: *The Story of Nannie Helen Burroughs*, New Hope Publishers, WMU®.

"Nannie Helen Burroughs was a petite woman with a presence that stretched around the world. She used her skills as an editor, writer, speaker, and teacher to gain an impact on the lives and living conditions of countless people, both nationally and internationally.

She once said, "It is a fact that God puts some great idea in every longing, human soul. At some point in our life—early or late, the earlier the better— we feel a trembling, fearful longing to do some good thing, something different to help some good cause."

That great idea came early for Nannie. She studied business and domestic science in high school and graduated with honors in 1896. At that time, African American women had few choices of employment. After several discouraging efforts at obtaining a job in the business field, Nannie developed a passion to open a school and prepare women to work for an honest living.

Looking back, Nannie said, "An idea struck out of the suffering of that disappointment that I would someday have a school here in Washington that school politics had nothing to do with and that would give all sorts of girls a fair chance to help them overcome whatever handicaps they might have. It came to me like a flash of light, and I knew I was to do that thing when the time came. But I couldn't do it yet, so I just put the idea away in the back of my head and left it there."

She worked in several positions, including serving as corresponding secretary of the Woman's Convention, Auxiliary to the National Baptist Convention, before opening the National Training School for Women and Girls in Washington, D.C., in 1909. Even while working in menial jobs, she kept her sights on improving opportunities for women. Nannie Helen Burroughs' entire life revolved around the pursuit of the God-given trembling, fearful longing to help African-American women.

In *The Story of Nannie Helen Burroughs*, a chronicle of triumph over seemingly impossible situations is the core of the story of one woman who sought after God, cared for His people, and made a tremendous impact for His kingdom."

From *The Story of Nannie Helen Burroughs*

Summer 1920

As social injustices and crimes against African-Americans became more common, Nannie joined forces with male and female leaders of her time to raise awareness and combat the mistreatment. During the 11th biennial National Association of Colored Women (NACW) conference, Nannie and several other African American women leaders met with Booker T. Washington at Tuskegee Institute to discuss lynching and women's right to vote. She and a few of the women from NACW also worked to prevent lynching with the Commission on Interracial Cooperation, which was composed of white women from protestant churches and other groups. Later that year, she joined Margaret Murray Washington (wife of Booker T. Washington), Mary McLeod Bethune, and other NACW women in founding the International Council of Women of the Darker Races in hopes of improving the overall lives of women of darker races.

Nannie also saw the church as an important tool in educating and rallying African American women for causes such as this. In her annual message, she urged women to organize or join suffrage clubs in their congregations. Meanwhile, she worked with many Republican groups to achieve the same goal.

Until the 1930s, most African-Americans identified with the Republican party for its ties to Abraham Lincoln and the emancipation of slaves, and Nannie worked with numerous political groups affiliated with the Republican party such as the National League of Republican Colored Women, which she helped pioneer in 1924 after the 19th Amendment passed in Congress allowing women to vote. She also worked with various religious groups, the Association for the Study of Negro Life and History, the NAACP (National Association for the Advancement of Colored People) and the National Association of Wage Earners, a group she founded in 1920 to improve working and living conditions of domestic service workers. As long as Nannie lived, she fought against social inequality and encouraged others to do the same.

LESSON SUMMATION

This lesson has taught us how the teachings of the Bible and the nature of God demand that we act to correct injustice. We have discovered that Israel's covenant with God required them to treat the poor fairly and seek to relieve injustice. We have been encouraged to use our own experiences and history to fuel our determination to cry for and carry out justice in our world.

DAILY DEVOTIONS

LESSON SIX
JUSTICE IN THE NEW TESTAMENT

The laws of God call us to remember the poor and strangers because of God's nature and mercy. This week we will review a New Testament account of Judgment Day that emphasizes the importance of justice in our lives. Each day, remember to thank God for His justice, His mercy, and His loving guidance in your life.

DAY ONE
MATTHEW 25:31–46
Read the entire passage, and compare the words of the King to the righteous "sheep" with His words to the "goats."

Write down your thoughts.

DAY TWO
MATTHEW 25:34–40

What did the King reward the sheep for doing?

To whom did they reach out?

To whom did the King say they were really ministering?

DAY THREE
MATTHEW 25:31–40

List the descriptions given of those who were said to be the same as the King—"the least of these."

Is any information given about how they came to be who they were and where they were?

How does this compare with what the poor of Judah required of their neighbors?

DAY FOUR
MATTHEW 25:41–46

What did the King condemn the "goats" for doing?

How did the goats respond when they were accused?

From whom had they really turned away?

DAY FIVE
MATTHEW 25:31–46

Reread the entire message. Consider your responses to the above questions, and write some ways you can better serve and love God by reaching out to the needy.

Write down how you will carry out your plan.

KEEP YOUR EYES ON THE PRIZE

NEHEMIAH 6–7

VITAL VERSES

"But they were scheming to harm me; so I sent messengers to them with this reply: 'I am carrying on a great project and cannot go down. Why should the work stop while I leave it and go down to you?" — NEHEMIAH 6:2–3

KEY TERMS

Prize: The spoils of war (Jeremiah 21:9) or something won in an athletic contest. Paul used it as an image for salvation (Philippians 3:14), the imperishable nature of which he compared with perishable wreaths (made of laurel leaves, parsley, celery, etc.) desired by the athletes of ancient Rome and Greece (1 Corinthians 9:24–25).

Games: Paul frequently used the metaphor of sporting events. He spoke of running a race (1 Corinthians 9:24–27; Galatians 2:2; 5:7; Philippians 3:14) and fighting a good fight (1 Timothy 1:18; 2 Timothy 4:7).

Crown: Symbolizes the final reward of Christians (2 Timothy 4:8; James 1:12; 1 Peter 5:4; Revelation 2:10).

It takes steady nerves and a fighter to stay out there. From the moment you walk into the stadium, you block out everything and everybody, until you get the command to start. I could only hear the cheers when the race is over." These are the words of Wilma Rudolph, the first American woman to win three gold medals in a single Olympiad. At the summer Olympics of 1960 in Rome, she won gold medals in the 100-meter dash, the 200-meter dash, and the 400-meter dash. A Black female born into a poor family in the South, she overcame the crippling effects of polio, which attacked her at age nine. How did she do it? By God's grace, with her eyes focused on the prize, she blocked out everything and everybody to win this and future victories.

Who determines your daily priorities? What takes your attention away from the great work that God has assigned to you? What or who has distracted you from focusing on your life purpose? In the game of life our opponents are those who do not understand our calling to lift high the name of Jesus Christ through our words and actions. The team cannot reach its full potential unless *you play your part*. We lift Him up to draw the world to abundant and eternal life in God through faith in Jesus Christ.

The world offers its lures and distractions. Your mission on this side of eternity is to let your light shine and offer the refreshing waters that will give restoration to those who now drink from broken and leaking cups. The race demands your full strength and will to endure. Block out everything and everybody that keeps you from the prize, the high call of God in Christ Jesus. *Keep your eyes on the prize!*

Take some time to read the Scripture for this lesson, Nehemiah chapters 6 and 7. (You may skip the list of names in chapter 7 if you want!)

Nehemiah and the people were quickly approaching the finish line—about to complete the restoration of the walls and gates. The last touches were being put on the twelve gates so that they could be hung. There must have been a growing sense of peace and satisfaction that came with knowing that they had been faithful to the task despite obstacles that at first seemed impossible to overcome. The reward for their faithfulness was within their view. But their enemies had not given up yet.

SATAN ON MY TRACK: NEHEMIAH 6:1-3

Sanballat and company changed their game plan; they began to focus their attention on blocking Nehemiah, rather than the builders. Why pick on Nehemiah? Without Nehemiah, the builders had the same probability of finishing the walls as the Chicago Bulls had of winning an NBA championship after Michael Jordan's retirement: slim to none. The enemies shifted their strategies from physical attack to mind games. They sent Nehemiah an invitation to attend *peace talks*, or a diplomatic dialogue, in the nearby village of Ono.

What were these guys up to? On the surface, the suggestion of a peace negotiation might seem to be a good thing. But it would have taken several days for Nehemiah to get to and from the meeting location. The village of Ono was located more than 20 miles northwest of Jerusalem. Should he go to Ono? Oh no, Nehemiah would not risk a work stoppage by the wall builders. He listened to the voice of God within him and discerned that they intended to harm him. His carefully worded and truthful response, which has become the basis of countless sermons, was divinely given: "I am doing a great work and I cannot come down." Who or what seeks to draw you away from the great work God has assigned to your hand?

If these guys had the right motive for a meeting, why did they not consider Nehemiah's needs to stay in Jerusalem and manage the building project? Why did they not hold the meeting after the project was completed or change its location to a place more convenient for Nehemiah? As time passed and additional invitations were sent to and turned down by Nehemiah, the true intention of his opponents was revealed. How should a person respond when the true agenda of others is hidden? Wait on God, and their true intentions will be exposed.

TRYING TO HOLD ME BACK: NEHEMIAH 6:4–9

The fifth invitation for a meeting was brought to Nehemiah by the servant of his opponents. The letter that came with the message was left unsealed to frighten Nehemiah with the prospect that its contents might be public knowledge. This letter, in the wrong hands, could have led to Nehemiah being charged with high treason for planning a rebellion against the rule of Persia. A story like this had caused King Artaxerxes to stop the project years ago (Ezra 4:8–23). The enemies wanted the gossip mills to roll and spin a false tale about Nehemiah and Israel's motives in restoring fortifications around Jerusalem. Their lies about Nehemiah were as follows:

- Nehemiah was rebuilding the walls of Jerusalem in order to start a war for independence from Persia.
- He was in the process of making himself King of Judah.
- He had prophets lined up to prophesy that there is a King in Judah.
- Geshem had verified the story (Nehemiah 2:19; 6:1).
- Word of the revolt was about to reach his boss, Artaxerxes, King of Persia.

Out of "genuine concern," they suggested he confer with them to work out a solution to this crisis. Yeah, right! Where? In Ono. Oh, no.

Walls around ancient cities were used both to defend and to launch attacks against one's enemy. Near Jerusalem lay Egypt, which was free from Persian rule and lately had been giving fits to the Persian army. They would welcome Israel as an ally and assist them in battle for independence. Many in Israel prayed that God would send a new king to sit on the throne of David. Was Nehemiah that king? Sanballat and company were shrewd and calculating. They mixed lies with enough truth to make them believable.

FALSE ACCUSATIONS: NEHEMIAH 6:5–9

Nehemiah knew better, but what was he to do? As always, he feared God and not human beings. He stood his ground, confronting their lies with the truth. His "house was in order," for he had done his homework by having the project preapproved by the king. He told them and publicly announced to all who would hear (everybody with an ear was probably listening) that this was another trick to frighten them. The rumor that the letter sought to ignite was fabricated in the ungodly minds of his opponents. Nehemiah lived his life with an integrity that left no grounds for assault. His motives were not selfish; he was motivated by his love of his land, his people, and his God. God gave him the right words at the right time.

Nehemiah returned to his wireless connection (prayer) to the God of the universe crying, "Now strengthen my hands." These words of Nehemiah remind me of the words my mom would say when her patience had run out, and she was about to give me a paddling. Her words, "Lord, give me strength," should be listed in a book called, *Famous Sayings of Black Mothers.* When you talk about character assassination, we can understand Nehemiah's pain, weariness, and frustration. The only way to survive is to cry out, "Lord, give me strength."

SCANDALIZE MY NAME: NEHEMIAH 6:10–14

Nehemiah visited the house of Shemaiah the prophet. Shemaiah should have had a sign in his yard stating, "False Prophecies for Sale," since he and others like him were more interested in financial gain than honoring their high calling as prophets of God. For reasons that aren't explained, Shemaiah was confined to his house. He gave Nehemiah the story that Nehemiah's enemies planned to kill him that night. "Let's hide out until this thing blows over," Shemaiah suggested. He knew an ideal location— inside the temple building, the house of God. Now, Jews were allowed to seek asylum in the temple area, but it was a sin by Jewish law for Nehemiah, a layperson, to enter the building where only priests were permitted to go (Numbers 18:5–7).

Nehemiah saw through this attempt to entrap him. He used his God-given wits and took the moral high ground. He knew that a leader must consider not only his own safety but also the morale of the people he leads. He knew it would be wrong to let his people see their leader running and hiding from an enemy. He also knew God's law prohibiting laypersons from entering the temple building, where the holy of holies resided. He feared God more than possible death. God showed Nehemiah that Shemaiah was lying. "Tobiah and Sanballat had hired him . . . to intimidate me so that I would commit a sin by doing this, and then they would give me a bad name to discredit me" (Nehemiah 6:12b–13).

Again Nehemiah prayed. He left his enemies Tobiah and Sanballat and the false prophets they hired in the hands of God. Nehemiah remained faithful to God and focused on the prize—the joy of completing the great work assigned to his hands by God.

FEAST ON GOD'S REWARD: NEHEMIAH 6:15–19

God, through Nehemiah and the builders, accomplished the great work in 52 days. For all time, Nehemiah would be the model of a wise, determined, faithful, and God-fearing leader. God gave the people a vision through Nehemiah, and the people worked faithfully with him to make God's plan for their dream a reality. When we lead out under God's command, we too will be victorious.

When the word of their achievement reached their enemies, those enemies had to acknowledge that God had done a great work through the Jews. Their former confidence in their own strength vanished. God had done it again. When we are faithful, though the battle is long, God does the same for you and me.

We also see that Tobiah seemed to have many of the important people of Judah under his thumb. The nobles wanted Nehemiah to give Tobiah a break—he was not as bad as all that. Perhaps he really wasn't all that bad—just under the influence of Sanballat. The Scriptures do not tell us. We do know that he and his son were related by marriage to leading families there. Though the Jewish leaders testified to his good character, Nehemiah stated calmly that he was receiving threatening letters from Tobiah.

SECURE THE WORK AND REWARD THE FAITHFUL: NEHEMIAH 7:1–4

Israel must first embrace spiritual restoration before it could experience the true worship of God and dedicate the wall. In the meantime, Nehemiah put in place leaders and guards to secure the city and protect its residents.

John T. Porter, pastor emeritus of my former church in Birmingham, said: "We are either going into a storm, in the midst of a storm, or coming out of a storm. It is a truth worth repeating." We must remain alert.

Nehemiah's brother, Hanani, had served in the critical role of securing Nehemiah's assistance in restoring the wall. He was faithful and God fearing. The passage tells us that Hanani and Hananiah were put in charge of the city. Many scholars say that Hanani and Hananiah are variations of the same name, which means "God has been gracious." Nehemiah rewarded his brother's faithfulness. If we remain faithful, God will reward us. For great work, God grants great rewards. Be faithful. Keep your eyes on the prize!

The rest of chapter 7 is a list documenting those who had returned from captivity to reestablish the city (Nehemiah 7:5–73). Few were living in the city while the work was being done. Most lived in surrounding settlements and towns. When the walls and gates were finished, the people cast lots to decide who would live in the city after it was secure. One in every ten was chosen to live in the holy city, while the rest stayed in their own towns (Nehemiah 11:1–23).

REFLECTIONS ON THE STORY

Why was Nehemiah targeted in the game plan of Sanballat and company?

They knew that he was the chief motivator of Israel's team. Nehemiah knew that God was well able to see them to victory. His main role was to get his team to stick to their divine plan. Even in life today, the most valuable players in God's plan take the most heat. Often when we have a significant plan in mind, we catch heat, and the heat grows more intense as we get closer to our goal.

Though we take heat, if we are steadfast in our trust in God, what will happen to us? (See Jeremiah 17:7–8.)

Are you on God's team and in God's game plan? In what specific ways is God using you?

Rewrite Jeremiah 17:7–8, personalizing it by putting your name in it instead.

What were the tactics of Nehemiah's opponents?

They tried to *divert his attention away from the work* with "peace talks." He saw that their intention was *to harm him*. They *lied* to and about him and tried to start a false rumor of Nehemiah's plot to rebel against the king. They worked through false prophets, using *fear* in an attempt to entrap him.

How did Nehemiah handle these tactics?

Nehemiah relied on God to give him the right words, to help him make the right decisions, to reveal his enemies' real intentions, and to uncover their plots.

His opponents wanted Nehemiah's responses to be based on fear and personal ambition.

If he had given in to those temptations, what would have happened to the work?

Instead, Nehemiah was seeking the good of others. He loved God and his people.

When these tactics of God's opponents challenge us, what spirit does God give us?

Diversions, poor decisions, persecution, and all-out attacks are used to keep us from our main task as Christ followers.

Consider the following terms, and put the correct one in each of the blanks below.

A. Diversions   B. Poor decisions   C. Persecution   D. Attacks

_____ are what capture our attention and keep us from our goals. They can be something as simple as watching too much television. They can be as complicated as keeping busy doing good but not checking with God to see if that is the good you were called to do.

_____ are often made when we decide to choose to do what clearly conflicts with the Word of God for temporary pleasure or benefit. At other times, the choice is between two or more things that are both good.

_____ happens when situations and people are used to stop, hinder, slander, deceive, lie about, or destroy the work, people, purpose and/or plan of God for God's people.

_____ happen when we are rejected, made to suffer, and threatened because we imitate, obey, and fear God (as Christians through faith in Jesus Christ).

Have the above devices ever hindered your spiritual progress? Give an example.

Evil keeps pulling out of its hat the same old set of tricks. Our job is to be spiritually dressed in the whole armor of God and alert to the task. Let me say from experience and study that women are most often attacked where it hurts us the most, in the areas of our relationships and finances.

Have you found that to be true in your life or in the lives of women you know? Give an example.

Those relationships include spouses, children, siblings, parents, friends, church members, and co-workers. Every relationship must be directed by our understanding of the will of God for us.

Our financial stability is affected by several issues, including lower wages based on race and gender. Often in Black married couples, both partners must work to maintain financial stability. Black women are often single or single with children, thus they have to make their dollars stretch farther. At times we make poor decisions related to financial planning. How can we deal with these problems? Commit your finances and financial planning to God, make a budget and stick to it, analyze why you buy things you can't afford to impress people you do not like, and exercise self control. If you have your finances together, keep on doing what you're doing. Pray for those of us who need to get our act together.

In studying Nehemiah, we uncover key qualities that can lead to victorious Christian living. What are some of the qualities that you admire in him?

The qualities that you admire might include the way Nehemiah lived out his calling, exercised wisdom, lived and spoke the truth, was committed to prayer, was faithful to the Word of God, and feared God. These same traits help young and old alike to lead more successful lives.

As a review of Nehemiah's qualities, fill in the blanks with the appropriate terms:

A. The Call of God   B. Wisdom   C. Truth

D. Prayer   E. The Word of God]   F. The fear of God]

_____ is a divine selection to fulfill the plan of God. Some individuals are selected for special vocations to carry out God's plan. Every believer has been selected for salvation through faith in Christ. Our vocation is carried out in the exercise of our spiritual gifts (Ephesians 4:1–16).

_____ begins with the proper awe and reverence for God. It provides principles for daily living (Proverbs 1:1–7).

_____ is the nature of God and makes God "constant, permanent, faithful, reliable" (Isaiah 65:16; Jeremiah 10:10). Jesus makes known to the world the reality that God made known to Him (John 8:26). Jesus is the way, the _____ , and the life (John 14:6).

_____ is conversation and communion between God and people. God communed with Adam (Genesis 3:9–12), Abraham (Genesis 15:1–6), and countless others throughout Scripture.

_____ is the inspired revelation of God's will and purpose. For Nehemiah, it was the Law of Moses. Jesus became it and dwelt among us (Psalm 119:11; John 1:1).

_____ is awe that a person should have before God (Proverbs 1:7; Ecclesiastes 12:13). It is characteristic of "true religion" and manifested in how we live and treat others (Psalm 34:11–14).

Nehemiah quickly discerned the unrighteousness of the prophets, such as Shemaiah. He knew and obeyed the Law of God. False and selfish prophets exist in abundance today. Many Blacks have been victims of false prophets like Jim Jones and David Koresh. We must be students of the Word.

Julia Brodner, an expert on a past Montel Williams show, said that cults exist for three reasons: the desire for money, power, or sexual gratification of the leader and/or his or her followers.

How do these desires compare with Nehemiah's service and Christ's ministry?

How can we identify false prophets? (See Matthew 7:15–20.)

What should prophets say? What should they not say? (See 2 Timothy 4:1–5.)

Just as Christ did, Nehemiah noted the faithfulness of the builders and promoted them. He remained alert and secured the city.

Do you take time to commend the faithful?

Looking at the places of concern in your life, what steps are you taking to secure the walls?

What can African Americans do to secure the walls of protection around our communities?

What can the church do?

What rewards will God give those who faithfully follow His will and example?

How wonderful it will be to hear our Savior say, "Well done, good and faithful servant! You have been faithful with a few things, I will make you ruler over many things." Our salvation is based on faith in Christ alone. Our crown of life will be rewarded based on our stewardship of His gifts to us.

CORETTA SCOTT KING

Kaylin Brown (Birmingham, Alabama; daughter of worship artist Ingrid Irons Brown and Pastor Cedric Brown), responds with her impressions of Coretta Scott King:

> "A perfect example of an overcomer," Kaylin writes. "Most recognize her as the wife of the profound preacher and civil rights leader Dr. Martin Luther King Jr., [but] Coretta also aspired to be a musician, was a famous singer, and a strong leader herself.
>
> "Mrs. King grew up in the 1930's during the Great Depression. At the age of 10, she and her brother had to pick cotton to help make ends meet for her family. At one point she was picking 200 pounds of cotton a day, just to earn 7 dollars. Although at that age Coretta

may not have known that her family was in poverty, she knew that she played a part in their wellbeing.

"She attended Mount Tabor A.M.E. Zion Church where her mother was the pianist and Coretta often sang solos.

"Coretta took her education very seriously. She was high school valedictorian and afterward studied at New England Conservatory of music, on scholarship.

"As a wife, she chose to invest herself in her marriage and family, including raising her children, but she also served a key role in the civil rights movement, alongside Dr. King. Throughout Coretta's life journey, she faced many obstacles. Working alongside her husband brought forth hatred and persecution toward her family.

"I can imagine the fear of how others would respond to the work to which she devoted her life. Mrs. King and three of her children were arrested at a South African embassy in Washington D.C., for protesting against South Africa's segregation laws. Her entire family was dedicated to supporting equality all over the world. The Kings went on missions to Africa, Latin America, Europe, and Asia.

"In 1968, when Dr. King was assassinated in Memphis, Tennessee, Mrs. King not only had to deal with the loss of her husband, but also with the responsibility of raising four children on her own. I wonder if she ever asked God, 'Why?'. She had strived to be an encourager to others but she needed encouragement. At that moment, she could have given up. She had plenty of reasons to discontinue the job God had given her to do. Yet Coretta King maintained her service in the African American communities and continued to be the civil rights activist she knew that she was called to be. After regaining some balance in her life, God refocused her to a new chapter in life. He allowed her to incorporate her gift of music into the civil rights movement by performing Freedom Concerts.

"The lesson to take away is to persevere through hard times. Nehemiah 4 explains how the Jews were criticized for trying to rebuild the wall of Jerusalem. The Scripture goes on to explain how, instead of retaliating on those who persecuted him, Nehemiah prayed. Because of this, the Lord blessed the Jews for being faithful in what He told them to do.

"I believe we can relate to Nehemiah and Mrs. King. As a maturing young adult, there are many goals I hope to accomplish in my lifetime. In between accomplishing goals, there will be setbacks. There will also be discouragers—'naysayers' that would love to see me or you give up on the work God has placed on our hearts to do. The truth of the matter is that any true work of God will prosper. All we have to do is keep our minds on the ultimate prize of making God's name great."

LESSON SUMMATION

From the moment we decided to follow the way of Christ, we have been rewarded with His presence and power to live faithful and loving lives under God. The moment we decided to follow Christ, our names were written in the Lamb's book of life. We have a guarantee of our heavenly reward through the precious and miraculous ministry of the Holy Spirit. We have a wireless connection to the God of the universe, who calls us to the throne of grace. If you stumble and fall, reach out to God; He will take you by the hand, heal your wounds, and lead you on the path from earth to heaven. Sometimes the load will get so heavy that God will lift you and your load above and beyond the obstacles that your opponents have set for you.

These obstacles will include diversions, persecution, lies, entrapment, and fear. But take God's precious hand, use wisdom, fear only God, speak and live truth, order your steps in God's words, know that God has brought you out of darkness into His marvelous light, and pray always. Our faithful God will restore your power, give you the wings of an eagle, make you walk without growing weary, run without fainting (Isaiah 40:28–31). For we are more than conquerors because of the might of God (Roman 8:37–39). The crown we receive will never perish for it is the crown of life. Keep pressing on!

⏤Daily⏤Devotions

LESSON SEVEN
RULES FOR WINNING THE CHRISTIAN RACE

This week we will use the lens of the New Testament to discover principles for winning the Christian race. We will focus on Philippians 3:1b to 4:1. Here Paul addresses a teaching of Jewish believers that all male followers of Christ must be circumcised. Paul proclaims that salvation is obtained not through any matter of the flesh, but through faith in Jesus Christ.

DAY ONE
DON'T RELY ON YOUR GOOD WORKS OR POWER
Philippians 3:2–6

Paul had relied on his religious heritage, birthright, and strict adherence to the Law as a "Hebrew of Hebrews." What do you rely on to get you into heaven? Your good works or religious heritage? We are not saved by our works but by faith, and we do good works as a result of that faith. Today, rejoice in the fact that you do not have to rely on your own works to win the Christian race.

Write the reasons you are thankful for this reality.

DAY TWO
RELY ON YOUR RELATIONSHIP WITH CHRIST
Philippians 3:7–9

All Paul had was worthless in comparison to knowing Christ Jesus as his Savior. Rejoice in the privilege of knowing Christ as your Savior and Lord. Rejoice in the fact that you have obtained the righteousness of Jesus Christ, our Savior and Lord. Jesus through God is the maker, maintainer, and pathfinder on the road we run.

Write down the reasons that you are thankful for this reality.

DAY THREE
EMPOWERED BY GOD HIMSELF, RUN WITH PATIENCE
Philippians 3:10–11

Daily in our race with Christ we grow in the knowledge of Him. To know Christ requires fellowship, communication, worship, praise, and prayer. This grows out of our love for Him and His love for us. We are willing to suffer trials because of our association with Him. We can endure by the power of God — it is so great that through it Christ rose from the dead! Rejoice in the knowledge that this power is yours.

Write down the reasons that you are thankful for this reality.

DAY FOUR
KEEP YOUR EYES ON THE PRIZE
Philippians 3:12–13

None of us have reached full maturity in our faith. We only have one thing to do—keep the focus of our whole being on reaching the Savior. Rejoice in the knowledge that you have to do but one thing—focus on Jesus.

Write down the reasons that you are thankful for this reality.

DAY FIVE
KEEP PRESSING ON
Philippians 3:14–16

Hold fast—your aim is to fulfill the call of God on your life. Your reward is heaven. The prize is to live forever with Christ. Rejoice in the knowledge of God's eagerness to reward you with the crown of life.

Write down the reasons that you are thankful for this reality.

THE LOVE OF GOD RESTORES

NEHEMIAH 8–10

VITAL VERSES

"Then all the people went away to eat and drink, to send portions of food and to celebrate with great joy, because they now understood the words that had been made known to them."—NEHEMIAH 8:12

"Those of Israelite descent had separated themselves from all foreigners. They stood in their places and confessed their sins and the wickedness of their fathers."—NEHEMIAH 9:2

KEY TERMS

Love: The Old Testament speaks of God's love in terms of covenant. God's steadfast love proves His faithfulness to His covenant to love, bless, and protect Israel. Israel's love is proven as the people honor and obey the Law of God. The New Testament speaks of God's love as shown in the sacrifice of His Son.

Joy: The Old Testament speaks of the joy found in following the Law of God (Psalm 1:1–2). The New Testament refers to the joy found in a relationship with Christ and the commandment to abide in God's love through obedience (John 15:10–11). This joy is present despite circumstances.

Feast of Tabernacles: This feast, one of three major festivals of the Jewish faith, took place on the 15th of the month of Tishri (late September to early October) and commemorated God's preservation of the children of Israel during their wanderings in the wilderness after exodus from Egypt.

Book of the Law: The Torah, the "instruction," the first five books of our Old Testament.

God loved you before the foundation of the world (Ephesians 1:3–4). God sent His Word, Jesus Christ, in human flesh and asked us to believe, repent, and receive. Inspired people of God wrote down the record of His love. These love letters, the Holy Scriptures, are for us to read and respond to in obedience to the covenant of love. Why do we neglect this magnificent record of a faithful God who is love? When we read and understand that we are unfaithful, will we repent, recommit, and follow more closely?

African Americans and especially African American women claim to love Jesus. Do we love God enough to regularly devote ourselves to the study of God's Word? When we study and understand, we are confronted with its truths. Do we ignore any signs of unfaithfulness in ourselves? If we say that we have not sinned, we lie, for everybody sins and falls short of the glory of God. When we do sin, do we repent and commit to following Christ more closely?

When we follow our shepherd closely, He will guide us to quiet waters and green meadows, and our souls will be restored. This restoration will bear fruit in our lives and strengthen our churches and communities. We will experience the joy of the Lord. Joy in the Lord is what gives restoration power.

Take some time now to read the main Scriptures for this lesson, Nehemiah chapters 8, 9, and 10.

We will end our study as we began it, remembering the magnitude of God's love for Israel and for us. This section of the book is not part of Nehemiah's memoirs, but is said to be written by "the Chronicler," who is also said to have collected the books of Chronicles. This part of the story shows us the ideal response to an encounter with the Word of God. Each response of the Israelites produced an increasing amount of joy. They read and understood the story of God's steadfast love and their unfaithfulness. They saw how they had neglected the requirements of the Law. They repented of their ancestors' and their own disloyalty to the Sinai covenant. They renewed their vows and increasingly obeyed God. The result was the joy of restoration.

The Sinai covenant marked the beginning of the special relationship between the nation of Israel and its Lord. God's love was unwavering and His faithfulness constant, but Israel had been unfaithful, often pursuing other gods and priorities, imitating nations that did not know the true God. Once more, God expressed His unending love and ceaseless compassion through the reestablishment of the protective walls around the Holy City. When we are wrong and God is love, how should we respond?

RESPONDING TO GOD'S LOVE: NEHEMIAH 7:73B TO 8:3

These verses summarize what takes place in Nehemiah 8:4–8. Israel longed to understand and respond to the Law of God and the story of God's love—but, of course, that is past human ability to fully understand. This inability should not prevent us from experiencing it as fully as we can on earth. Israel determined to do this by requesting a reading of the Law, which holds the stories of God's devotion and gives the requirements of faithful covenant partners. Ezra conducted the reading on the holy day of the Jewish New Year (the first day of the seventh month) on the east side of town in the square near the Water Gate, which was near the temple holy place (Leviticus 23:23–25; Numbers 29:1–6). Gathered were women, men, and children old enough to comprehend the teachings delivered that day.

Spellbound, the congregation listened at full attention with hearts opened, ears attuned, and minds prepared to receive loving yet stern words from God. Don't you wish you could have been there? It would have challenged our modern short attention spans. The event was a six-hour Bible study and praise service, and no one worried about whether or not the stove was left on, what Sister Susie was wearing, when the preacher would finish, or whether they would get out of the service in time to catch the kickoff of the game. They came for a word from God and didn't leave before He got through saying what He had to say. What would happen if the church folk of today so deeply and earnestly desired the Word of God?

SOURCE OF JOY: NEHEMIAH 8:4-8

Ezra and 13 assistants brought the scroll and then stood together on a raised platform built especially for the occasion. Ezra opened the Holy Writ, and the crowd as one stood up in reverence for the Law. Seeing their thirst for the Law, praises to their great God spilled from Ezra's lips. They responded, with hands lifted in anticipation, with a twofold amen: "So be it! So be it!" The Holy Presence was so real that they bowed down, with faces to the ground, and praised God with their whole being. Awesome! They got happy *in anticipation* of the great word from their Great God.

The platform members began to read the Word of God. But what is the Word of God without a clear understanding of its meaning to and for us in our times? So the Levites fulfilled their role as teachers. They shared its meaning and significance with the people. The people began to weep bitterly as they understood the Law of God and saw how their own lives fell short of the requirements set by it. In times like that, sorrow and weeping are appropriate. How else can we respond when we consider who God is and what God has done, is doing, and will do for us?

WORD OF GOD: NEHEMIAH 8:9–12

Godly sorrow and genuine repentance never leave us in our grief. The leaders reminded the people that there is a time for everything, and this day they had gathered for a celebration, not a funeral. They were to enjoy the special food and drink they had prepared and to share with those who had nothing to eat. They were not to let the devil take away their joy! They left rejoicing, ready to share their food and spread their joy. The season for joy is found in one of the Vital Verses for this chapter, Nehemiah 8:12: "Then all the people went away to eat and drink, to send portions of food and to celebrate with great joy, because they *now understood the words that had been made known to them*" (*author's emphasis*). Their joy was so great that it could not be contained but had to be proclaimed! Surely some sister said, "You shoulda' been there."

FRUIT OF REVIVAL—OBEDIENCE: NEHEMIAH 8:13–18

Knowledge and understanding should lead to obedience. On the second day of the seventh month, when others had returned to their homes, (listen closely) the family heads, Levites, and priests gathered to soak in God's Word. They discovered while studying that they had neglected to properly celebrate the Feast of Tabernacles since the time of Joshua. During that feast, they were to live for seven days in booths (tents, shelters) like those made following their ancestors' deliverance from Egyptian bondage (Leviticus 23:33–44). They understood and obeyed the Law. They built their tabernacles on their roofs, in their courtyards, near the Temple, and near the Water and Ephraim gates. Their obedience to the Law led them into tremendous joy.

FRUIT OF REVIVAL—REPENTANCE: NEHEMIAH 9:1–37

Some 23 days had passed, and the revival continued. The family heads and religious leaders had been soaking their thoughts, feelings, and spirits in the purifying and convicting truth of God. This encounter with the love letters that document God's sometimes subtle, sometimes awesome expressions of devotion to them caused them to recognize their sins of faithlessness. The Israelites repented, turned around, and went back in the right direction—toward God.

- They genuinely expressed sorrow with fasting. Their custom when fasting was to wear sackcloth and put ashes or dirt on their foreheads (v. 1).

- They exercised a holy lifestyle by setting themselves apart to serve their God, refusing to imitate their foreign neighbors (v. 2).

- They prayed, acknowledging that in every generation of their nation's existence, God's steadfast love had been shown and His deliverance and protection had been provided (vv. 5–15).

- They joined with Ezra in a heartfelt and beautiful prayer, confessing their sins and the sins of their ancestors (vv. 16–37).

When you look back at your life, where have you seen proof of God's steadfast love?

FRUIT OF REVIVAL—RESTORATION: NEHEMIAH 10:30–39

The covenant vows were renewed. The Jews recognized that their pursuit of other gods, split loyalty, and imitation of the peoples that surrounded them had left them in distress and bondage—physical bondage because they were at the mercy of the Persians, mental and emotional bondage because they felt shame and reproach for abandoning God, and spiritual bondage because they had failed to return to total devotion and obedience to God. They cried out to God for deliverance and committed themselves to a renewed devotion to God's Law.

Their joy in God began to swell up in their being as they heard, understood, and repented. Each of these things lifted the heavy load of sin, guilt, and shame. Their recommitment included separation from the peoples around them with no intermarrying of foreigners to the Israelite faith, commitment to maintain the house of God, refusal to buy or sell on the Sabbath, and fulfillment of their promise to leave their fields for the poor in the seventh year. Their joy was not just the joy of God; it was the joy of restoration of a broken relationship—restoration by God.

The Israelites' recommitment was based on their best understanding of what God required of them. Israel experienced restoration through obedience and by the power of God. We, too, can reclaim and take back what is gone—our relationship with God—and repossess the full joy of God. We, too, can be restored.

What does God require of you? Are you meeting and maintaining those requirements?

At last, the people were ready, and the new fortification of the holy city could be dedicated.

LESSONS LEARNED

The writer of this portion of the Book of Nehemiah wanted us to know that true restoration must include an encounter with the Holy God. That encounter was possible because Israel willingly gave themselves over to God's presence, power, and principles. They let go of their will and surrendered to the will of God for their lives. The result was unspeakable joy.

Let us look at some specific things we can learn from them about community, church, and personal spiritual restoration.

- **Absolutely surrender.** Total surrender, not self-sufficiency, is required for spiritual restoration. Only when we recognize we are lost can we be found; only those who confess their weariness find rest; and only when we acknowledge our sickness will we be healed (Luke 5:31–32; Matthew11:28). Have you accepted your need for absolute dependence and trust? Surrender to God is not a one-time event. Each day we must deny self and put on Christlike ways.

- **Crave the Word of God.** Studying the Word of God brings a fuller understanding of the will of God; this alone is reason enough for great joy. Most of the books that comprise the Old Testament had not yet been compiled and the New Testament had not been written when Nehemiah's story occurred. Many of their faith stories were passed on by word of mouth. This reading by Ezra was special and rare. No wonder the people craved a word from God.

For restoration to occur and continue we must crave the Word of God. What then is the Word of God? Read the Scriptures below and give the answer in your own words.

2 Timothy 3:16–17

Acts 4:31

John 1:1

- **Correctly understand the Word of God.** The Ethiopian eunuch read the words of the prophet Isaiah, but he did not fully understand them (Acts 8:30–31). God sent Philip to interpret and lead him to faith in Christ. In our lesson, the people were able to grasp the meaning of the Law because their teachers, the Levites, helped them to grasp its meaning. We can know the Word of God ourselves because the Holy Spirit serves as our teacher and interpreter (1 John 2:26–27). We must study the text within its context, however.

For example, what does Scripture teach us about the rights of one person to enslave another? (See Ephesians 6:5–8.)

This text in context speaks to the circumstances of persons almost 2,000 years ago. American slave masters, to justify and retain human bondage, used this same text to control their slaves, our ancestors. Slaves of faith, like Frederick Douglass, saw that the total context of the Scriptures, the life and teachings of Christ, the Law, and stories of Moses condemned human bondage. Many Scriptures, such as Exodus 3:7–10; Deuteronomy 23:15–16; Jeremiah 34:9–10; John 8:34–36; 1 Corinthians 7:21–23; Galatians 3:26–29; and the book of Philemon, teach us the larger view of how God sees slavery.

We must be students of the total Word of God. Why? (See 2 Timothy 2:15.)

Once we understand the Word of God within its context and through the filter of the Living Word—Jesus Christ—we can then handle the Word correctly. Only then can we hope to apply the text to ourselves without robbing it of its meaning. Slaves in America who were believers clung to the passages of Scripture that affirmed their dignity, God's mercy, and His power to liberate. Slave owners would use passages such as Ephesians 6:5–8 to suggest that God approved of slavery. Who was right and who was wrong? The slave owners did not have a correct understanding of that passage. They interpreted the Bible to make it say what they *wished* it said.

We know that many have used Scripture inappropriately to confirm their own version of the truth.

Why? (See 2 Peter 2:1–3.)

• **Reverence the Word of God.** Consider the example of the people in Nehemiah 8:5.

How should we always approach Scripture?

When you read the Bible, approach it reverently, with respect. Let God speak to you through the holy words of the Bible, and never try to twist those words to your own wishes. When you read the Bible, always remember the following steps:

   Step 1: Prayerfully ask for God's guidance.

   Step 2: Be open to the Spirit of Truth.

   Step 3: Consider the text in its context.

Step 4: Learn the historical situation that surrounds the text.

Step 5: Apply that Scripture to your own life.

What was the response of the people when Ezra blessed the greatness of God? (See Nehemiah 8:6.)

Give one example of the greatness of God in your life.

• **Repent.** The word *repentance* comes from the word *shub*, which means "retracing one's steps in order to return in the right way."

What was the Jews' initial response when hearing and understanding the Word of God? (See Nehemiah 8:9.)

Looking at their lives in contrast with the demands of God, they were convicted and grieved by their sins. Chapter 9 of Nehemiah recounts the story of God's faithful and steadfast love despite the sins of Israel. Rather than following the laws of God, they sought happiness in imitating nations that did not fear their God. The result was that they found themselves separated from the God who was the source of their peace, love, and joy.

What can African American women and all peoples learn from their story?

Have we imitated others in their search for the "good life"?

- **Remember.** One of the most critical keys to Israel's survival as a people under God was their tradition of passing down their faith stories. At the time this story was written, they passed on their faith by remembering their ancestors' stories.

What portions of African American history encourage you to be faithful to God?

RENEW THE COVENANT OF LOVE

Later in Nehemiah, the leaders and the community signed an agreement to renew their covenant with God. The covenant of Moses at Mount Sinai outlined the demands of God's Law.

What is the purpose of the Law? (See Romans 3:20.)

Who is our only hope for forgiveness, salvation, and righteousness? (See Romans 8:1–2.)

We believe in Jesus and, thus, we are saved. We live by the covenant of God written on the tablets of our hearts (Jeremiah 17:1; 2 Corinthians 3:3,6).

How is this contract fulfilled? Jesus states that we are to love. If we love God, every commandment will be fulfilled, for we will not love any people, place, or thing above God. We will not covet, bear false witness, or mistreat another human being.

Restoration will be complete when we love God and our neighbors in what way? (See Matthew 22:37–39.)

What was the chief failing of the church at Ephesus? (See Revelation 2:4.)

The Old Testament speaks of the standard of love for God and one's neighbor. For Israel, neighbors were those who lived by them (Exodus 12:4). Israel's community was made up of those who joined in covenant with the Lord God.

Who are a Christian's neighbors? Jesus, in His parable about the good Samaritan, addressed this question (Luke 10:29–37). All our fellow earth dwellers are our neighbors. This definition, then, includes our enemies. It is easy for us to point our fingers at others and question the genuineness of their love.

Do some African Americans carry within themselves unresolved racial hatred?

Christ calls us to love everybody—friends and foes. Ephesians 1:9–10 teaches us that God's ultimate purpose in Jesus Christ is to unite all nations and peoples under the lordship of Jesus Christ. We are called to love our enemies.

When we love, obey, and live in fellowship with Christ, what will be the result? (See John 15:10–11.)

Nehemiah 8:10 contains a well-loved phrase: "The joy of the _____ is your _____."

THE JOY OF THE LORD

Unlike the happiness that the world gives, God grants us joy that is found in union with Christ and peace with God. This joy of God gives us strength to overcome every obstacle in life. The joy of God gives us the strength to serve God. The joy of God gives us the strength to reach out to others who are spiritually and economically oppressed and depressed. The joy of God fortifies us to say no to temptation. Nothing the world has compares to the joy our relationship with God gives. The joy given is great, but ultimate joy will come when we live forever in God's presence.

Having the joy of God, what should we do? (See Nehemiah 12:43.)

How did God express the width, depth, height, and length of His love? (See John 3:16.)

How will you share your knowledge of God's love and joy with those who need restoration?

The people of Judah renewed their vows in a recommitment service (Nehemiah 9:1–6; 10:28–30). Let's commit together to share the news of our joyous restoration. Christians are under a covenant of love based on salvation through faith (Ephesians 2:12–19). Will you recommit to loving God first and foremost? Will you love with heart, soul, mind, and strength? Will you obey Him all the days of your life? Will you express your love for Him by loving your neighbor as you love yourself?

Do you know that God loves you? God has whispered His love for you in the rocky and calm times of your life. The Bible will show you in a thousand ways that God loves you. God has loved you since before your birth. God loved you before you knew to return that love. God's love will grant you joy.

Joy is what lets you smile in the midst of pain. Joy is what the world cannot give or take away. God's joy is your strength. Offer your life as a living offering to God. Proclaim all the joyous restoration found in God. Let your praise be heard far and wide from everlasting to everlasting.

EXPERIENCING MARGARET AIKENS JENKINS

(as told by author Sharon Norris Elliott)

"From the best seat in the house—balcony front row center—I experienced Margaret Jenkins for the first time. The three elegant women on stage at their places behind the microphones smiled and began to sway to the Hammond organ introduction.

"Mesmerizing the audience with their grace and their beautiful, floor-length pink gowns for the next hour and a half, the Ladies of Song captivated the audience with the message of their music. The perfectly blended voices of Margaret Jenkins, her sister Celeste Scott, and Robbie Preston sang of the

Lord. Something about Margaret's smile made me want to praise the Lord with her same exuberance.

The joy of such concerts weren't always a part of Margaret's life though. She had her share of tough times being raised as a "mixed-race" child. Her grandfather had done the unthinkable back in that day and had fallen in love with and married a "Negro" woman. Her father, extremely light-skinned, too, did the same. This prompted the family's move from Mississippi because, in the early 1900's, 'race-mixing' was not only intolerable but also could bring deadly consequences. Still, despite the hatred often spewed at the family, Margaret grew up as a happy little girl, but determined to see to it that as many children as possible would know they were loved.

It was precisely because of learning to stand up for herself in the face of vitriolic hatred that she became a woman to be experienced. When she made up her mind to do something, she did it. Both she and her sister had a strong love for children, so Margaret decided to open a school. Sadly, Celeste passed away of a massive heart attack while on stage performing. In Celeste's honor, Margaret forged ahead with the idea of the school and named it after Celeste. My chance to experience Margaret up close came when I secured my first teaching position at Celeste Scott Christian School (CSCS).

Mrs. Jenkins was known as 'Grandma' to every student. Discipline for serious infractions included a lecture from her (and harsher measures when warranted) in the name of Jesus, but every child at that school was absolutely convinced that he or she was loved. Joy rang out from every child enrolled—preschool through 10th grade—as every special holiday was accompanied by an all-out, full stage, gospel musical production. The students were taught by Margaret's example to love God, family, each other, and the world.

Although blessed with boundless energy even into her 80s, Mrs. Jenkins passed away a few years ago. Hundreds of former CSCS students returned from all across the country to attend her homegoing celebration. Joyously ringing in every heart was the chorus of the school's theme song that depicted the love and care 'Grandma' held toward every child:

'Walk a mile, for a child
Teach them how to pray each and every day
Take them by the hand and show them the way
Light the torch and save the children.'

LESSON SUMMATION

The love story between God and His children—His people—continues. The magnitude of God's steadfast love has been manifest in every generation. God's Word, when heard and understood, demands that we respond in obedient love. The people who had worked for the restoration of Jerusalem, by the end of the story, had heard God's Word (the Law), understood it, repented, and renewed their covenant vows. They found restoration as they lived faithfully in the will of God.

African Americans have been loved by God through every generation. Recognize that the mighty hand of God is able to restore all that we have lost and all that has been taken away. Daily by God's power, reclaim and live a joyously restored life. Pray for God's continued power to follow Nehemiah's example, and continuously offer others the refreshing and joyous water of spiritual restoration found in Christ.

We must love God with all our hearts, souls, minds, and strength. Looking back over your life from birth to this present moment, do you see that God has been there all the time? He never fails to bring restoration to His people. Restoration is to be found when we live in the love and joy of God.

⊙ᴅ Daily Devotions

LESSON EIGHT
LIVE OUT PERSONAL RESTORATION!

This week, our devotions will review the eight principles from Nehemiah that will produce personal and national spiritual restoration.

DAY ONE
Review the Vital Verses from Lesson One and Lesson Two of this study (Nehemiah 1:3; 1:4).

Principle 1: Know that you have been called to be restored. God has chosen you to fulfill your vocation as a woman of God.

Principle 2: Continue to rely on and utilize the power of prayer. Know that what we ask in faith according to His will shall be done.

Write down your thoughts and/or prayer:

DAY TWO
Review the Vital Verses from Lesson Three and Lesson Four (Nehemiah 2:4–5, 8b; 2:18).

Principle 3: Take leaps of faith, for with faith you can move mountains and uproot trees, transforming your life and your world.

Principle 4: Maintain unity by walking in God's will for your life. Pray for the unity of God's people and our people, so others will see we are followers of the Light and also be drawn to follow Christ.

Write down your thoughts and/or prayer:

DAY THREE

Review the Vital Verses from Lesson Five and Lesson Six (Nehemiah 4:8–9; 5:1, 5).

Principle 5: Put on your spiritual armor daily. Pray and build up spiritual attributes to help you bless those you love.

Principle 6: Cry out for justice by advocating and acting for justice. Treat others justly.

Write down your thoughts and/or prayer:

DAY FOUR

Review the Vital Verses from Lesson Seven and Lesson Eight (Nehemiah 6:2b–3; 8:12; 9:2).

Principle 7: Keep your eyes on the prize of the high calling of God in Christ. The prize is to live forever with God.

Principle 8: Order yourself in God's Word. Know that we fulfill God's commands by loving God first and foremost and loving one another as we love ourselves.

Write down your thoughts and/or prayer:

DAY FIVE
Read Nehemiah 8:10–12.

The rebuilders of Jerusalem were overcome with emotion when they realized they had reached a milestone in their restoration of the city and in their relationship with God. But the leaders urged them to celebrate—to have choice food and drinks, to share it with those who had none, and to have a party in honor of the restoring work of God in their lives. When you reach a milestone and feel God's restoring work in your life, remember to celebrate!

Write down your thoughts and/or prayer:

ONCLUSION

"And on that day they offered great sacrifices, rejoicing because God had given them great joy. The women and children also rejoiced. The sound of rejoicing in Jerusalem could be heard far away." —NEHEMIAH 12:43

The call to restore the walls was completed under the efficient, wise, and faithful leadership of Nehemiah. His willingness to go to Jerusalem was rewarded. The gracious hand of the Lord was upon him. Their covenant loyalty restored, the people of Israel joyfully dedicated the fortified wall and gates of their city. This proof of the steadfast love of God had relieved their shame, reproach, and distress. The celebration included great sacrifices. They sacrificed their choice animals in praise and thanksgiving for God's grace, love, and mercy.

The singers and players of cymbals, harps, and lyres gathered from their villages. After the Levites and priests ceremonially cleansed themselves and the people, the service of praise and thanksgiving began.

The leaders of Judah and two great choirs divided and circled the wall in opposite directions. Ezra, the scribe, went with one group and Nehemiah, the other group. When they met in the area near the temple, they conducted a worship service of a power and magnitude that had not been experienced in the land in more than a hundred years. The wall and gates of their city and their spiritual lives had been restored by God's power. Their joy was heard far away. Their rejoicing was a testimony to the work God can and will do as His people seek personal and corporate restoration.

After the work of restoration, Nehemiah returned to Persia to resume his place of service to King Artaxerxes. Later in the story, he returned to Jerusalem and took on another term as governor. He called the people again to be loyal to their covenant commitments. He again dealt with residents of Jerusalem who were loyal to his old enemies, Sanballat and Tobiah. Faithfulness to God is a constant battle. We must exercise spiritual disciplines and fight many battles. We rejoice in the knowledge that if we press on, God strengthens us by His might. We must keep our "hand on the plow and hold on."

The lessons we learned from this marvelous Book of Nehemiah can ignite our desire to remain loyal to God's covenant of love. The greatest love was shown us when God gave His only begotten Son that we may live our lives victoriously, testifying to the love we have found in Christ.

We have come this far by faith. Our people have triumphed over great adversity. We must follow our Lord, not the world. Our forebears showed us the way. Journalist and author Tavis Smiley gave us these words of truth:

> As Black Americans, we have to approach our legacies as if they are individual bricks in a wall. We cannot have a wall without those bricks and, without the wall, we're nothing but a mess of bricks waiting to be carted away. If you have a chance to examine the Great Wall of China closely, you'll see that the bricks, in and of themselves, are very ordinary. But as a collective unit, those bricks are one of the world's greatest wonders—and the only man-made wonder visible from outer space. As individuals we need to be dedicated and diligent about our actions that represent us a race to the rest of the world. We are headed in that direction, but we won't get there unless everybody considers their own legacy. We don't need anyone contributing a flawed

brick to our great Black American wall. So, what are you doing to deserve your place on the wall?

—TAVIS SMILEY, "Ten Challenges to Black America,"
How to Make Black America Better

Well said, brother Tavis. We must reclaim and take back our spiritual power. We must build and rebuild daily on our faith. We must recall and pass on our story of God's love. We must pass on our legacy. Each must secure her portion of the wall. We do it for God. We know that what helps our people makes our nation and world better. African Americans of faith believe that God's power is available to bring restoration. If we do, God will fight with us and for us. How will we be sustained in the heat of the battles? The joy of the Lord is our strength.

Each and every day God grants us the opportunity for restoration. Each and every day God allows the sun to rise. We should give our lives as our praise offering for the mercy, love, and grace in our lives. The door has been opened and the pathway is lit with the brilliant light of the Son. When we offer our lives, they will be a testament to the restoration available to anyone. Our joyous testimony will be heard even from far away.

NOTE TO THE LEADER

As leader of the group, you can set up a structure for the group Bible study that will make women comfortable and help them to share and to grow together as Christian women. Remember to pray for the women each week. Below is a list of things you will want to do regularly throughout the study. As you recognize other activities that would benefit your group, add to the list:

—— Encourage your group members to complete each week's lesson before the meeting. Point out that at the end of each lesson are five daily devotions, which can each be done in 5 to 10 minutes.

—— Complete each lesson yourself, remembering to identify areas of special interest to your group of women.

—— Help women to recognize God's power moving in their lives as they study Nehemiah. This study is not only to help women learn the Bible, but also to help them experience God's power to bring restoration in the lives of African American women today.

For each contemporary or historical figure highlighted in each of the lessons, ask your participants to consider:

Restorer's Story:
❑ What lessons can we glean from the life of this week's woman of faith?
❑ What do you most admire about her life?

LESSON ONE

Opening Prayer: *10 minutes*
Begin by asking the women to form groups of two or three. Ask them to share with each other one area of life in which they see the need for restoration, and to pray together for these needs. After about five minutes, pray yourself for the women present, praising God that these women are His chosen vessels for restoration.

Vital Verse & Key Terms: *5 minutes*
Read the Vital Verse for the week. To get feedback regarding the Key Terms, ask questions: What does this word or term mean to you? What new meaning has it taken on because of your study?

Group Discussion: *15 minutes*
Establish the setting for the Book of Nehemiah—explain the beginnings of the Babylonian captivity, the defeat of Babylon by Persia, and the gradual return of the Jewish exiles to Jerusalem. Ask the group:

____ What are some parallels between the experience of the Jews of Nehemiah's time and African Americans of our day? What are some ways they differ?

____ Why do you think Nehemiah, who was wealthy and successful in Persia, was so distraught at the news of his homeland?

Life Application: *15 minutes*
Ask the women for their response to the first few paragraphs of Lesson One. Ask the group questions, such as (adapt these for your group's specific interests):

____ What was your response to the first part of Lesson One, which repeated the phrase, "Our walls are torn down and our gates burned with fire"? Does the author's view match your experience of African American life?

—— Is the African American community in need of restoration? How?

—— Are the spiritual walls and gates that surround you and your family strong and fully secure? Are they under siege? What about your church? Your community?

Closing: *5 minutes*

Urge the women to make a list this week of needs for restoration in their world. Encourage them to let God open their eyes. Close with prayer.

LESSON TWO

Opening Prayer: *10 minutes*

Ask the women if God opened their eyes to any needs for restoration this week. Have a time of prayer requests for those needs, and spend time in prayer. Praise God for His willingness and ability to answer all our prayers.

Vital Verse & Key Terms: *5 minutes*

Read the Vital Verse for the week. To get feedback regarding the Key Terms, ask questions: What does this word or term mean to you? What new meaning has it taken on because of your study of this lesson?

Group Discussion: *15 minutes*

Nehemiah began his work of restoration with a powerful prayer to God. Ask the group what was significant for them about Nehemiah's prayer. Then lead the group through the seven attributes of

Nehemiah's prayer, illuminating each one with your insights and encouraging discussion:

1. He ran to the throne of God.
2. He recalled the attributes of God.
3. He resounded the faithfulness of God.
4. He repented of unfaithfulness to God.
5. He relied on the promises of God.
6. He resorted to the mercy of God.
7. He asked God to help him take the next step.

Life Application: *15 minutes*

Encourage the group to discuss the importance of prayer for restoration. How often do we pray for our loved ones, our community, and ourselves? What kind of actions do we believe God is willing and able to take? What kind of actions do we believe God will not take? If your group would enjoy this, encourage them to form groups and write their own prayer for restoration, using Nehemiah's prayer as a model.

Closing: *5 minutes*

Close with a time of prayer, an extended time if possible, giving women time to voice the prayers they wrote, or having a time of guided prayer using the seven attributes listed above.

LESSON THREE

Opening Prayer: *10 minutes*

Ask the women to find a partner and share what they do when they are waiting—in line, at the traffic light, in a beauty parlor. Do they pull out their digital device? Do they daydream? Do they get mad? Spend time in prayer, asking God to give these women the patience to wait on God and the boldness to act when the time is right. Praise God for the times He has proven faithful when we have taken the leap of faith.

Vital Verses & Key Terms: *5 minutes*

Read the Vital Verses for the week. To get feedback regarding the Key Terms, ask questions: What does this word or term mean to you? What new meaning has it taken on because of your study of this lesson?

Group Discussion: *15 minutes*

Nehemiah had to wait for the right time to take his leap of faith and ask the king's permission to rebuild Jerusalem's wall. Discuss the times of waiting in African American history. When were some times when waiting was a good thing to do? When were some times when making a leap of faith was necessary? Read the poem "The Mask" (included in Lesson Three), and discuss its meaning.

Life Application: *15 minutes*

Use the examples from the introduction to Lesson Three to discuss people God raised up at the right time. Ask the women if they know anyone who should be added to the list. Let them briefly describe a few of these people. Discuss the difficulty of waiting and the difficulty of making a leap of faith. Ask which is harder for them. Ask the question: If you are waiting for God to answer a particular prayer or show you something about your life destiny, what are you doing in the meantime?

Closing: *5 minutes*

Pray for each woman there, that God would give her discernment as she seeks restoration for herself and those around her. Pray that God would show each woman when to wait and when to leap.

LESSON FOUR

Opening Prayer: *10 minutes*

Ask the women to form groups of five or six. Have each group decide what is the single most important need for restoration in the African American community, and then pray about it. The catch is this: they can't pray until their group reaches unity and all agree on one thing to pray about. (Stop them after seven minutes if they haven't agreed.) Let each group share the most important need they identified.

Vital Verse & Key Terms: *5 minutes*

Read the Vital Verse for the week. To get feedback regarding the Key Terms, ask questions: What does this word or term mean to you? What new meaning has it taken on because of your study of this lesson?

Group Discussion: *15 minutes*

Read the quote from Susan Taylor in the introduction of Lesson Four. Ask the women if they agree. This lesson focuses on Nehemiah's efforts to unify the people so they could accomplish the task of restoring Jerusalem's strength. Ask the women to look at Nehemiah chapters 2 and 3 and mention some of the wise things he did to achieve this. (See the sections in the lesson subtitled *Keep Your Balance* and *Elements of a Unified Work* for some possible answers.)

Life Application: *15 minutes*

_____ Ask the group to describe some ways to work for unity in their church and community. In what ways is unity possible? In what ways is it impossible?

_____ How do Nehemiah's efforts remind you of the way the body of Christ, the church, should function?

_____ Does your prayer life include a prayer for the unity of the church with its many nations and peoples?

Closing: *5 minutes*

Spend some time praising God for His love and power, which enables us to bring about unity in our homes and our world.

LESSON FIVE

Opening Prayer: *10 minutes*
Begin by reading the Maya Angelou quote from Lesson Five. Then ask the women to share one reason they're glad God made them African American women. You could go around the group or let people volunteer to share, depending on your group members' confidence level. Pray aloud, thanking God for all the good gifts He gave to African American women.

Vital Verses & Key Terms: *5 minutes*
Read the Vital Verses for the week. To get feedback regarding the Key Terms, ask questions: What does this word or term mean to you? What new meaning has it taken on because of your study of this lesson?

Group Discussion: *15 minutes*
Summarize for the group the opposition Nehemiah faced and the methods he used to deal with that opposition. Note that Nehemiah was vigilant and had his people carry weapons at all times, and that this was enough to discourage his enemies from attacking.

Life Application: *15 minutes*
Ask the women to join with a partner, and have the partners share with each other how they deal with opposition. Have them each answer the question: Are you usually ready to fight it or reluctant to fight? Then lead discussion about how to deal with opposition. As Christians, we may feel that we shouldn't fight at any time. Ask: What are some times when it's right to fight? What are some lies that are told about and believed by African Americans? Discuss particular

lies about women, men, and children. What can we do to counteract these lies? Think about negatives attached to the term *Black*.

Closing: *5 minutes*
Pray for each woman present, that God would give her weapons of the spirit and make her strong on behalf of His cause.

LESSON SIX

Opening Prayer: *10 minutes*
Ask the women to briefly share their strongest image or memory from the civil rights movement. Pray, thanking God that He is not finished bringing justice and restoration to the Black community, and thanking Him that the women present have been called to be a part of that work.

Vital Verses & Key Terms: *5 minutes*
Read the Vital Verses for the week. To get feedback regarding the Key Terms, ask questions: What does this word or term mean to you? What new meaning has it taken on because of your study of this lesson?

Group Discussion: *15 minutes*
This week's lesson focuses on justice. Nehemiah discovered that some of the Jews in the community were taking advantage of the poor during a time of famine. Ask: In what ways were they taking advantage of the poor? (They were charging high interest, selling people into slavery when they couldn't pay, and confiscating land.) Discuss Nehemiah's response to this. (He spoke out against it, lent money to the poor at no interest, refused his governor's salary; as the leader he gave the people an example to follow.)

Life Application: *15 minutes*
Lead discussion using some of the following questions:

——— What are the most pressing justice issues for the African American community today? Compare these to the justice issues addressed in the civil rights movement.

——— Discuss the significance of poverty—how do people become poor?

——— What does the Bible say about believers' responsibility to the poor?

——— Is working to relieve poverty a justice issue or an act of mercy?

Closing: *5 minutes*

Thank God for raising African American people to be lovers of justice. Ask Him to show the women some practical ways they and their families can assist Him in bringing about justice.

LESSON SEVEN

Opening Prayer: *10 minutes*

Ask the women to share aloud their favorite athlete or sport and a trait that they admire about the athletes (besides being good looking!). Pray that the positive traits named—possibly strength, focus, endurance, discipline, and/or boldness—will be exemplified in their Christian race.

Vital Verses & Key Terms: *5 minutes*

Read the Vital Verses for the week. To get feedback regarding the Key Terms, ask questions: What does this word or term mean to you? What new meaning has it taken on because of your study of this lesson?

Group Discussion: *15 minutes*

In Lesson Seven, Nehemiah's opponents try various ways to distract him from keeping his "eyes on the prize." Ask the group to name three ways Nehemiah's enemies tried to distract him. Which of those do you think was most likely to succeed? How did Nehemiah resist?

Life Application: *15 minutes*

_____ Ask: What obstacles have distracted you from keeping your eyes on the prize?

_____ Make an outline of a garbage can on a piece of paper. Make a copy for each woman and ask her to write inside the outline the distractions that need to be thrown out of their lives.

_____ The author suggests that two areas where women most often experience trouble are relationships and finances. Ask: Do you agree or disagree? Discuss.

Closing: *5 minutes*
Pray for the women and their commitment to put away things from their pasts that hinder or block their fulfillment in Christ Jesus. Pray in particular for the things they have identified as hindrances.

LESSON EIGHT

Opening Prayer: *10 minutes*
Ask the women to get a partner and share one way they've seen God's power for restoration at work during the time of this study. After they've shared, lead the group in prayer, praising God for His continuous power and might at work in the life of each woman there.

Vital Verses & Key Terms: *5 minutes*
Read the Vital Verses for the week. To get feedback regarding the Key

Terms, ask questions: What does this word or term mean to you? What new meaning has it taken on because of your study of this lesson?

Group Discussion: *15 minutes*
When the work of rebuilding the wall and gates was finished, the people celebrated and renewed their vows to God. Using the three fruits of revival from the lesson, discuss the spiritual rewards of faithfully following through on God's path to restoration.

Life Application: *15 minutes*
Lead the group to discuss how Nehemiah's journey toward restoration can enlighten their lives, their churches, and the African American community. Consider questions like the following:

_____ What lessons from Nehemiah are key for us?

_____ What would happen if church folks today deeply and earnestly desired the Word of God?

_____ What part of the African American story encourages you to be faithful to God?

Closing: *5 minutes*
End this session with a prayer of praise for all God has shown each woman during this time of studying together. Thank God for the time to grow in love for one another. Praise God for His power to bring restoration. Reclaim the losses and thank God for the gains of our faith and our people. Covenant together to be restorers—to rebuild the walls and reestablish the gates that surround us, our families, our churches, and our communities. Ask each woman to commit to letting her joy and love for God be heard and seen, even from "far off."

BIBLIOGRAPHY

Achtemeier, Paul J. *Harper's Bible Dictionary.* San Francisco: Harper & Row Publishers, 1985.

Appiah, Kwame Anthony, and Henry Louis Gates, Jr. *Africana: The Encyclopedia of the African and African American Experience.* New York: Basic Books, 1999.

Bandstra, Barry L. *Reading the Old Testament: An Introduction to the Hebrew Bible.* Belmont: Wadsworth Publishing Company, 1999.

Barboza, Steven. *The African American Book of Values: Classic Moral Stories.* New York: Doubleday Dell Publishing Group, Inc., 1998.

Barclay, William. *The Gospel of Matthew: Volume 1.* The Daily Study Bible Series, revised ed. Philadelphia: Westminster Press, 1975.

Barclay, William. *The Letters of the Corinthians.* The Daily Study Bible Series, revised ed. Philadelphia: Westminster Press, 1975.

Brueggemann, Walter. *A Social Reading of the Old Testament.* Minneapolis: Fortress Press, 1994.

Buttrick, George Arthur, commentary ed. *The Interpreter's Bible: Volume III.* Nashville: Abingdon Press, 1952.

Coogan, Michael D., ed. *The Oxford History of the Biblical World.* New York: Oxford University Press, 1998.

Elliott, Sharon Norris. *Power Suit: The Armor of God for the Feminine Frame*. Birmingham: New Hope Publishers, 2010.

Felder, Cain Hope, ed. *Stony the Road We Trod: African American Biblical Interpretation*. Minneapolis: Fortress Press, 1991.

Felder, Cain Hope. *Troubling the Biblical Waters: Race, Class, and Family*. Maryknoll, NY: Orbis Books, 1990.

Getz, Gene A. *Nehemiah: Becoming a Disciplined Leader*. Men of Character. Nashville: Broadman & Holman Publishers, 1995.

Klein, Ralph W. *The New Interpreter's Bible: Volume III. The Books of Ezra and Nehemiah: Introduction, Commentary, and Reflections*. Nashville: Abingdon Press, 1999.

Stott, John R. W., ed. *The Message of the Sermon on the Mount*. Leicester, England: InterVarsity Press, 1972.

Tenney, Merrill C., general ed. *The Zondervan Pictorial Bible Dictionary*. Grand Rapids: Zondervan Publishing House, 1967.

Washington, Sondra. *The Story of Nannie Helen Burroughs*. Birmingham: New Hope Publishers, WMU®, 2006.

New Hope® Publishers is a division of WMU®, an international organization that challenges Christian believers to understand and be radically involved in God's mission. For more information about WMU, go to wmu.com. More information about New Hope books may be found at NewHopeDigital.com. New Hope books may be purchased at your local bookstore.

Use the QR reader on your
smartphone to visit us online at
NewHopeDigital.com

If you've been blessed by this book, we would like to hear your story.
The publisher and author welcome your comments and
suggestions at: newhopereader@wmu.org.

WorldCrafts℠ develops sustainable, fair-trade businesses among impoverished people around the world. Each WorldCrafts product represents lives changed by the opportunity to earn an income with dignity and to hear the offer of everlasting life.

Visit WorldCrafts.org to learn more about WorldCrafts artisans, hosting WorldCrafts parties and to shop!

WORLDCRAFTS℠

Committed. Holistic. Fair Trade.
WorldCrafts.org   1-800-968-7301

WorldCrafts is a division of WMU®.

RESTORE REFRESH RENEW!

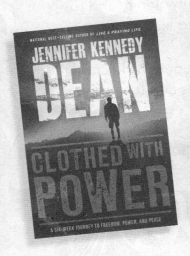

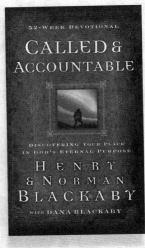

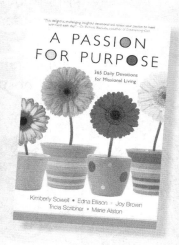

Clothed with Power

A Six-Week Journey to Freedom, Power, and Peace

JENNIFER KENNEDY DEAN

ISBN-10: 1-59669-373-8
ISBN-13: 978-1-59669-373-9
N134114 • $14.99

Called and Accountable 52-Week Devotional

Discovering Your Place in God's Eternal Purpose

HENRY & NORMAN BLACKABY

ISBN-10: 1-59669-214-6
ISBN-13: 978-1-59669-214-5
N084137 • $14.99

A Passion for Purpose

365 Daily Devotionals for Missional Living

KIMBERLY SOWELL, EDNA ELLISON, JOY BROWN, TRICIA SCRIBNER, AND MARIE ALSTON

ISBN-10: 1-59669-242-1
ISBN-13: 978-1-59669-242-8
N094137 • $16.99

Available in bookstores everywhere. For information about these books or our authors visit NewHopeDigital.com. Experience sample chapters, podcasts, author interviews and more! Download the New Hope app for your iPad, iPhone, or Android!

NEW HOPE
PUBLISHERS
Gospel-Centered. Missions-Driven.